D0778714

Creepy-Crawlies

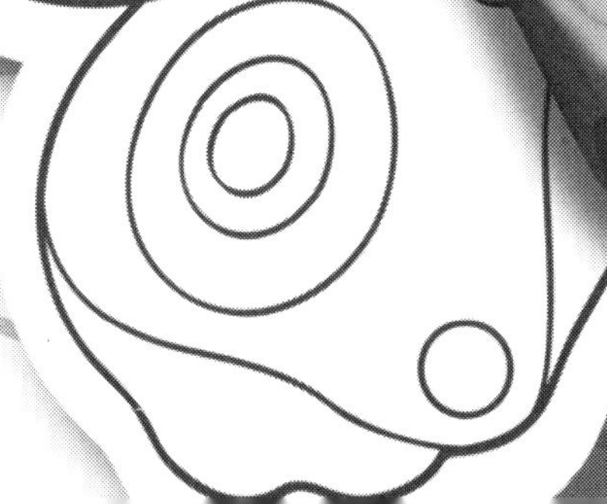

How to use this book

1. Trace the grid opposite. You can use any size paper as long as the grid proportions are the same as the one in this book. The grid squares will help you position your drawing and ensure that the different stages are correctly scaled.

2. Use a light pencil line to draw. That way you can erase the lines much more easily.

3. Copy the shapes in Step 1 and then add the new shapes in Step 2 and so on. As you add each step, your picture will begin to take shape.

4. When you have copied each step, erase the extra lines from the earlier step—to eventually reveal the final shape (as shown in the last step).

5. Now color in your finished picture.

As you become more confident, you might find that you no longer need the grid squares. You might want to add your own finishing touches to the illustrations, such as background plants, to create a scene.

Caterpillar

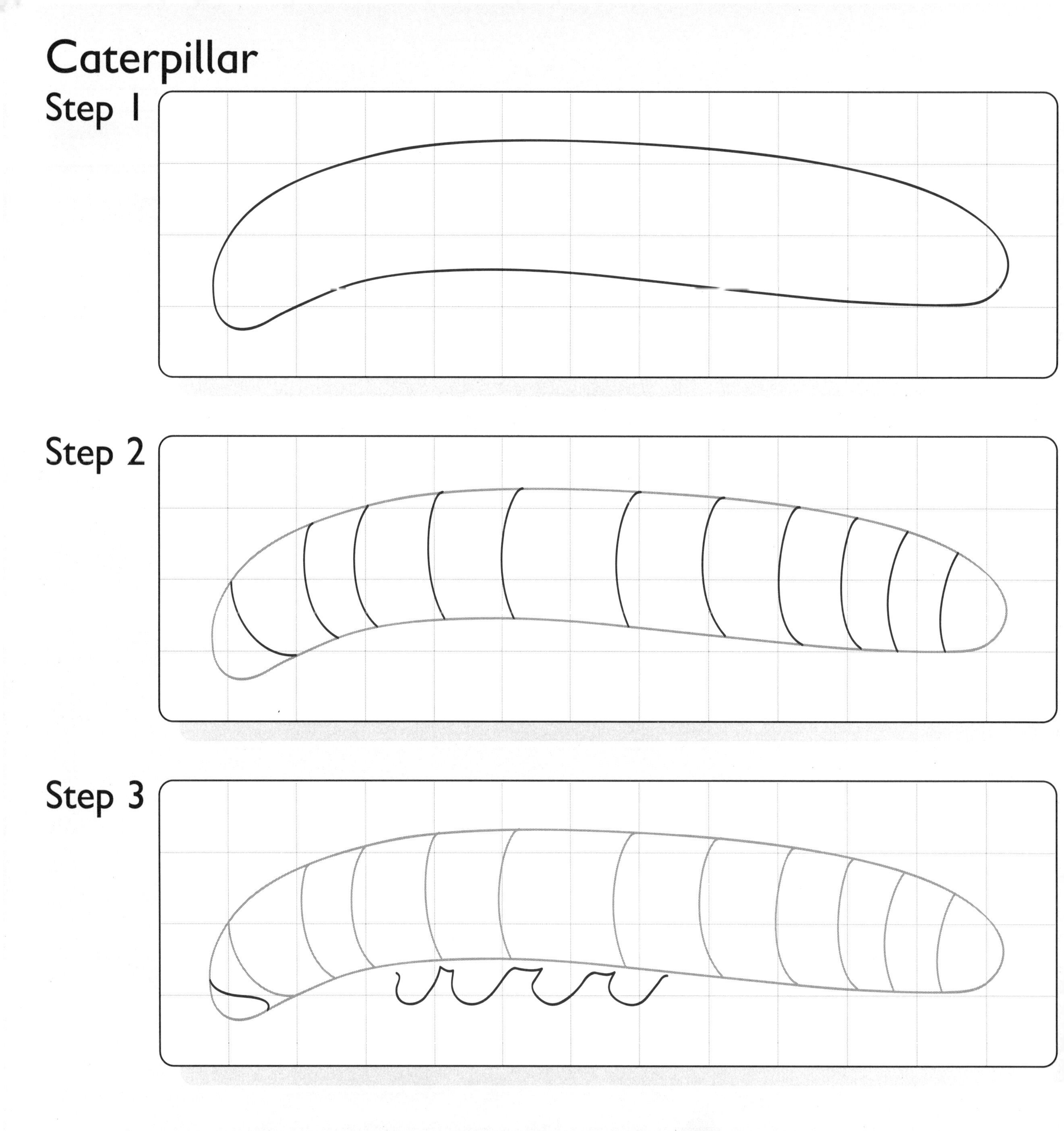

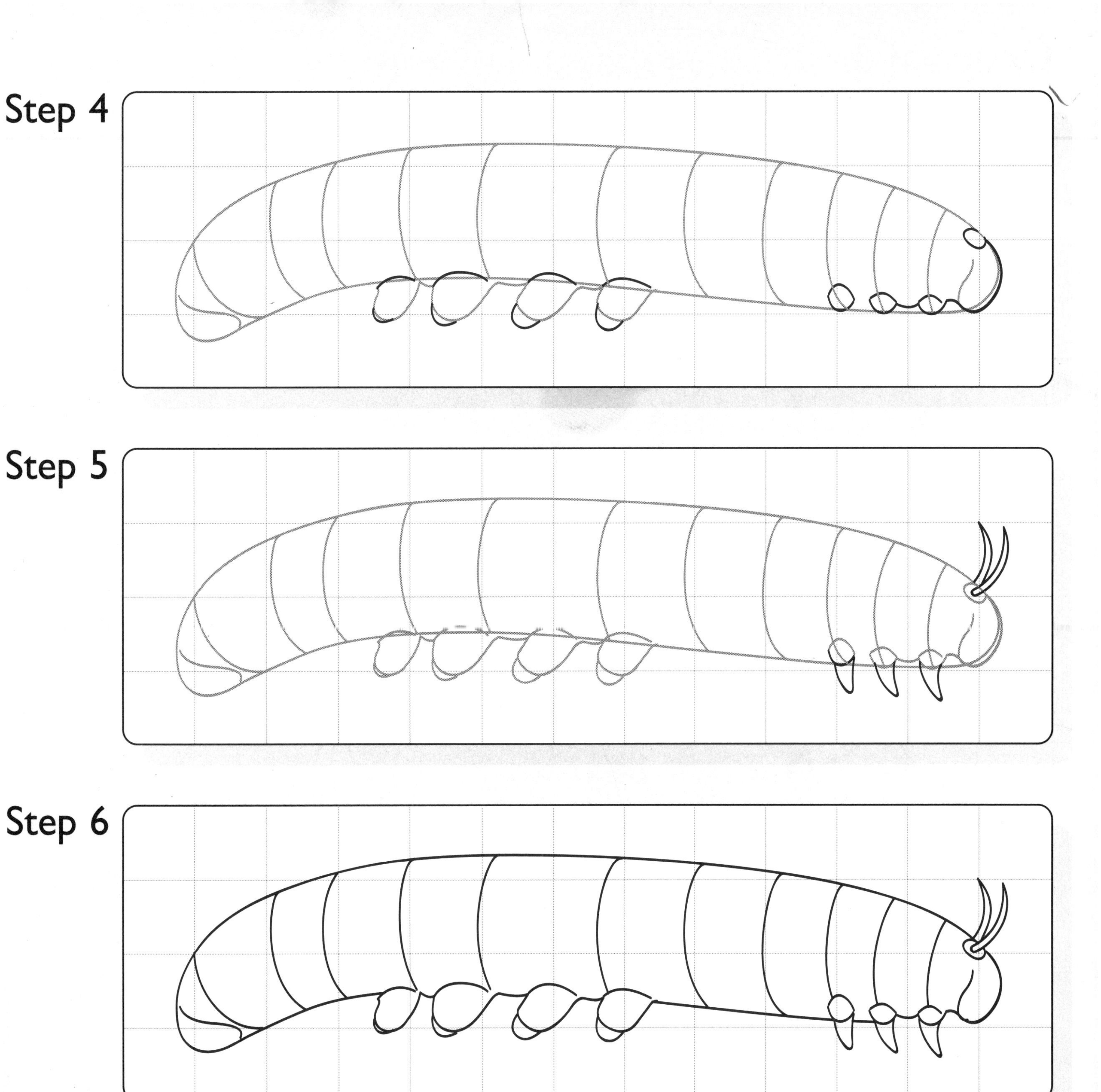
Step 4
Step 5
Step 6

Dragonfly

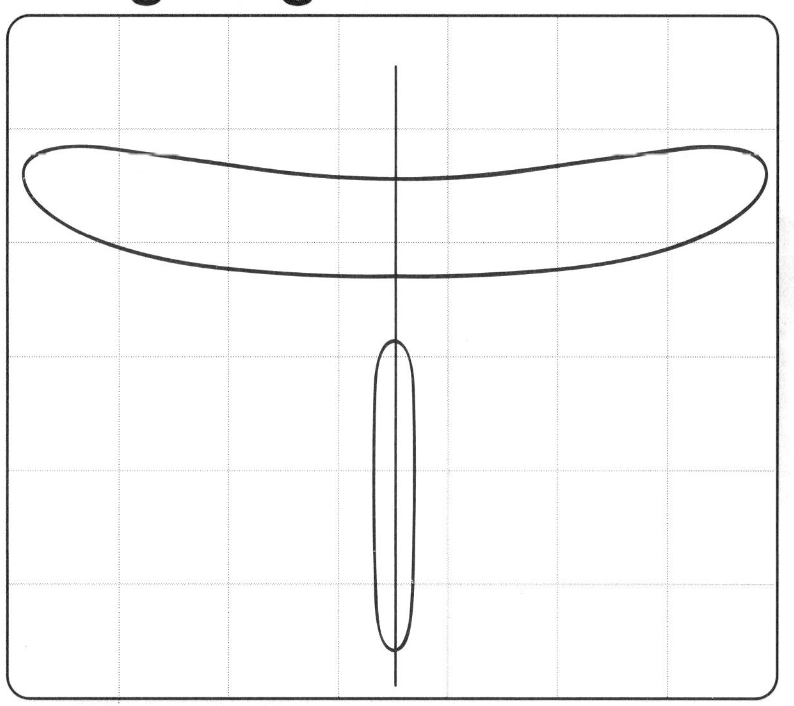

Step 1

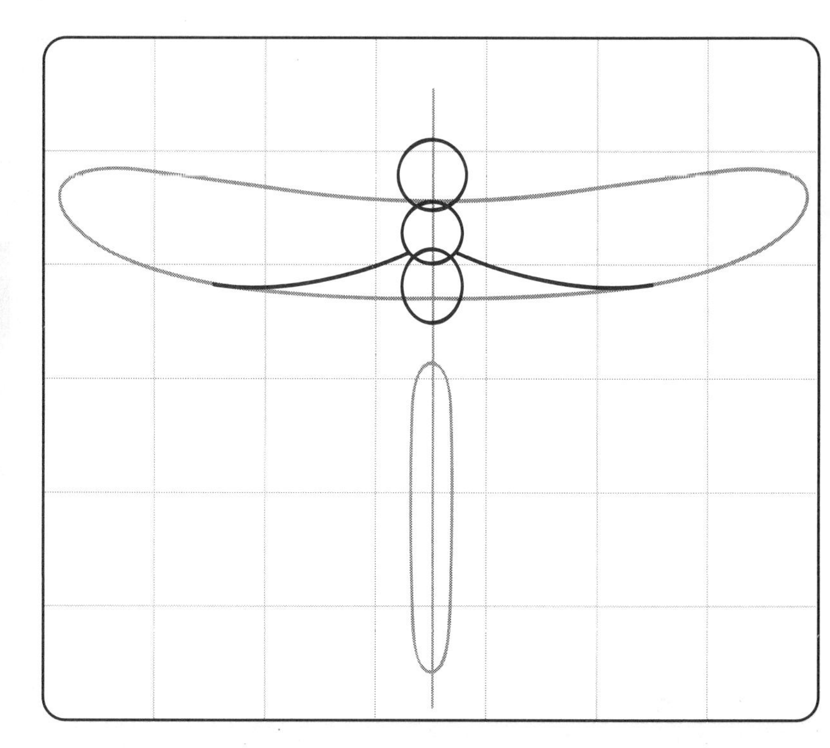

Step 2

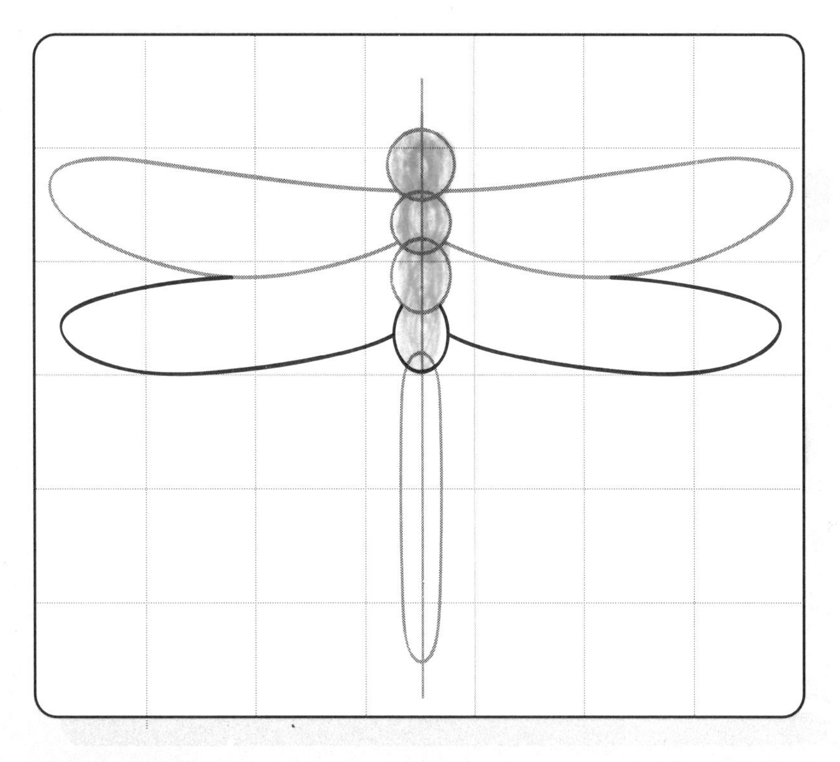

Step 3

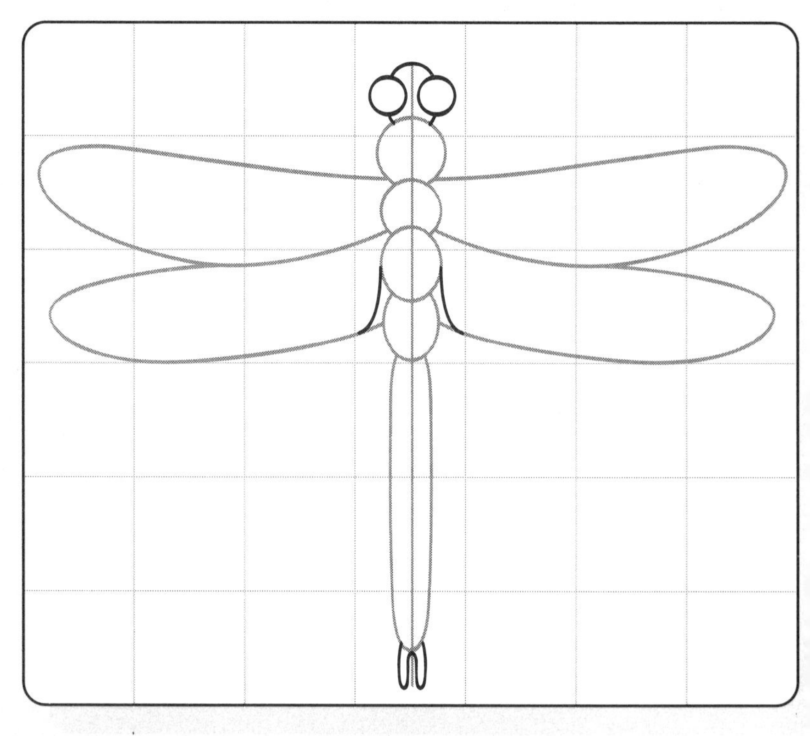

Step 4

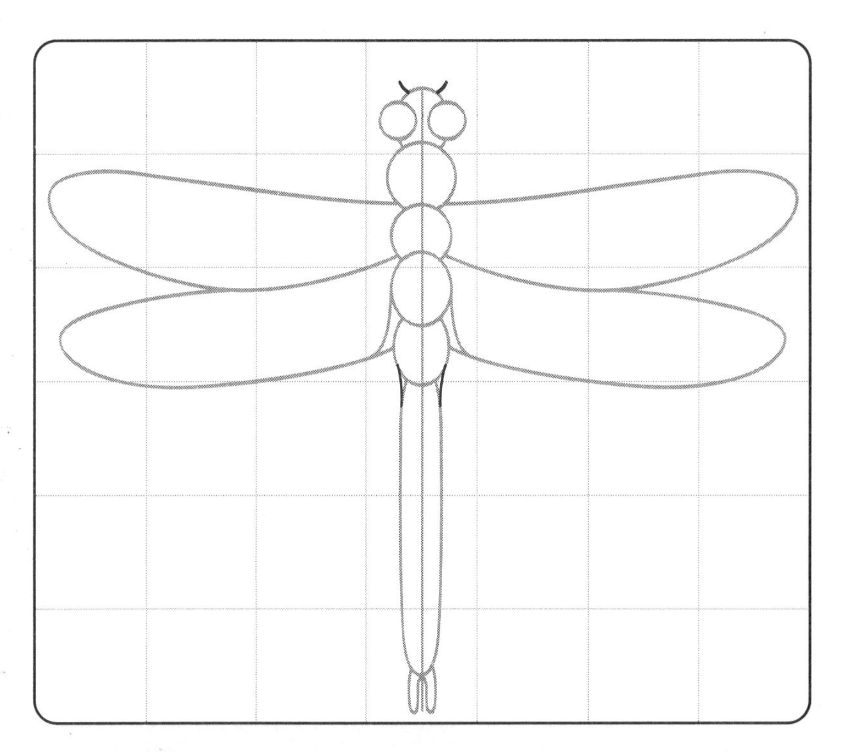

Step 5

Step 6

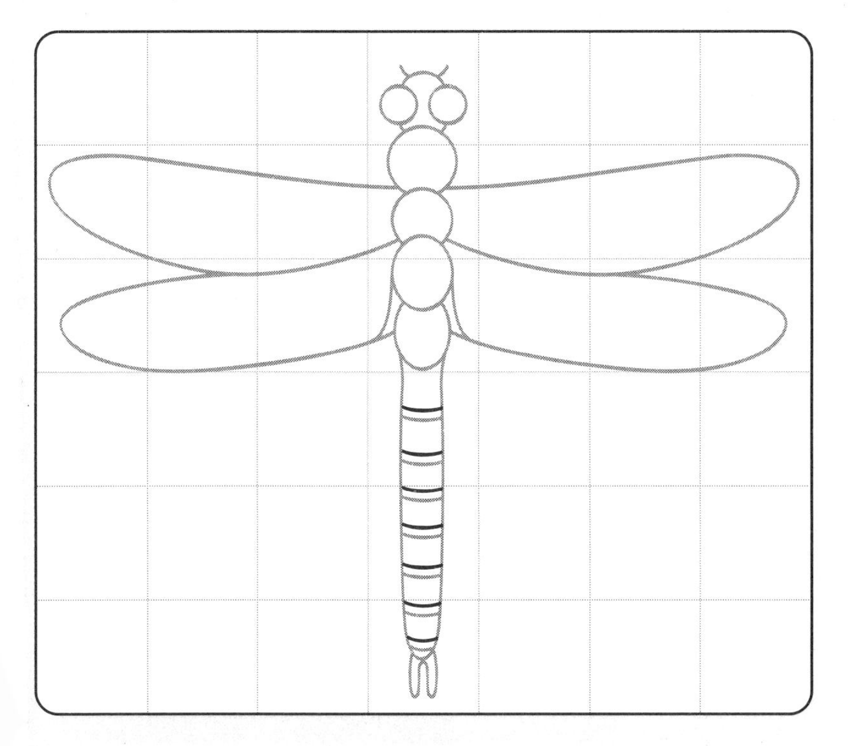

Step 7

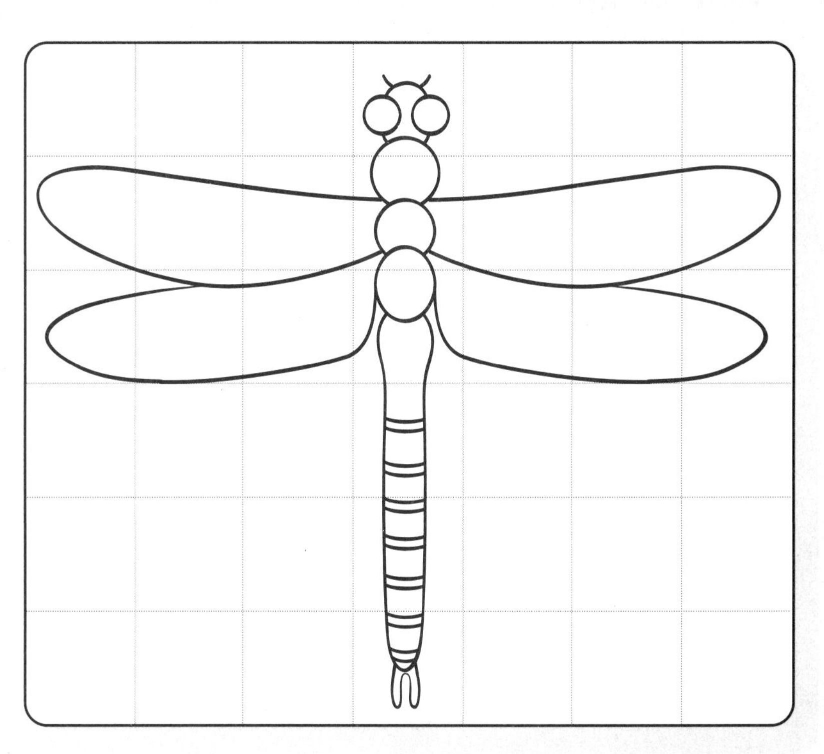

Step 8

Scorpion

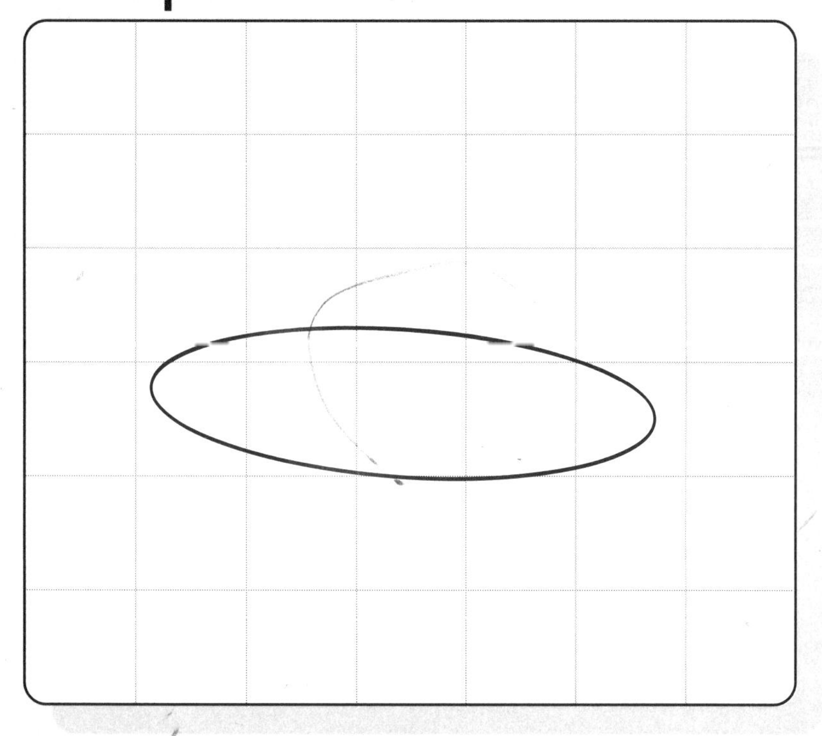

Step 1

Step 2

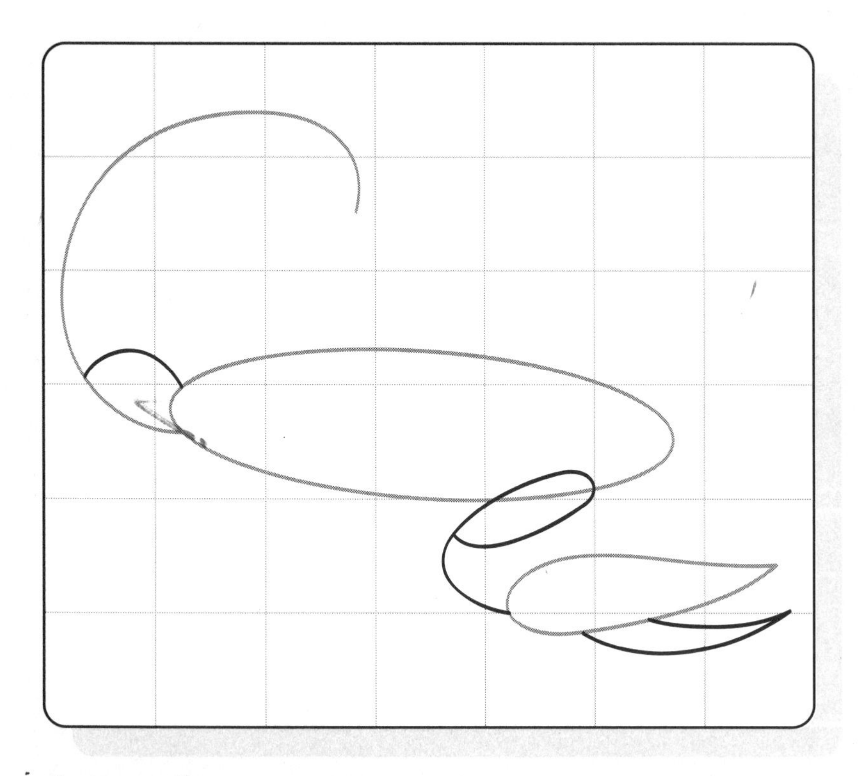

Step 3

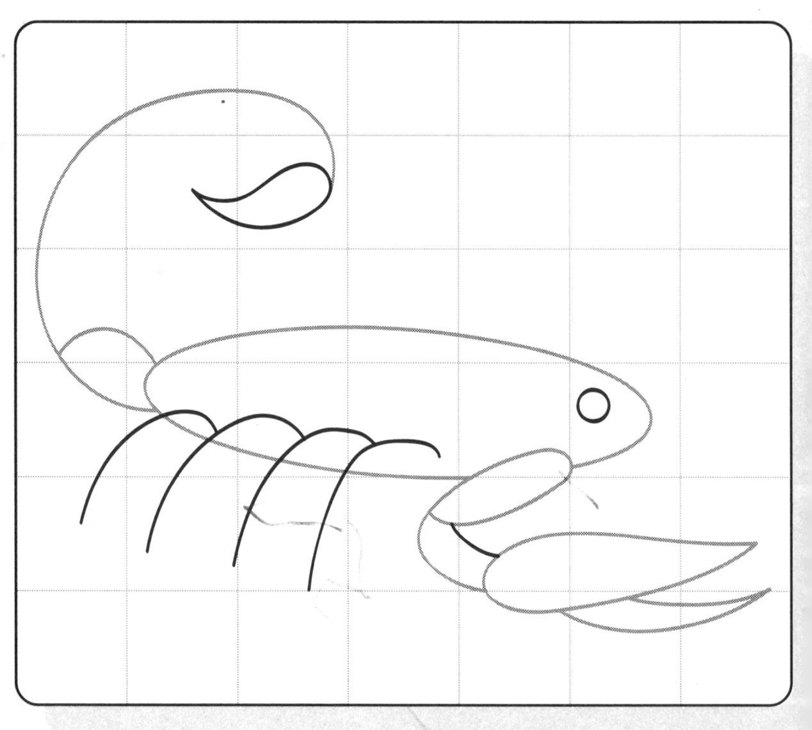

Step 4

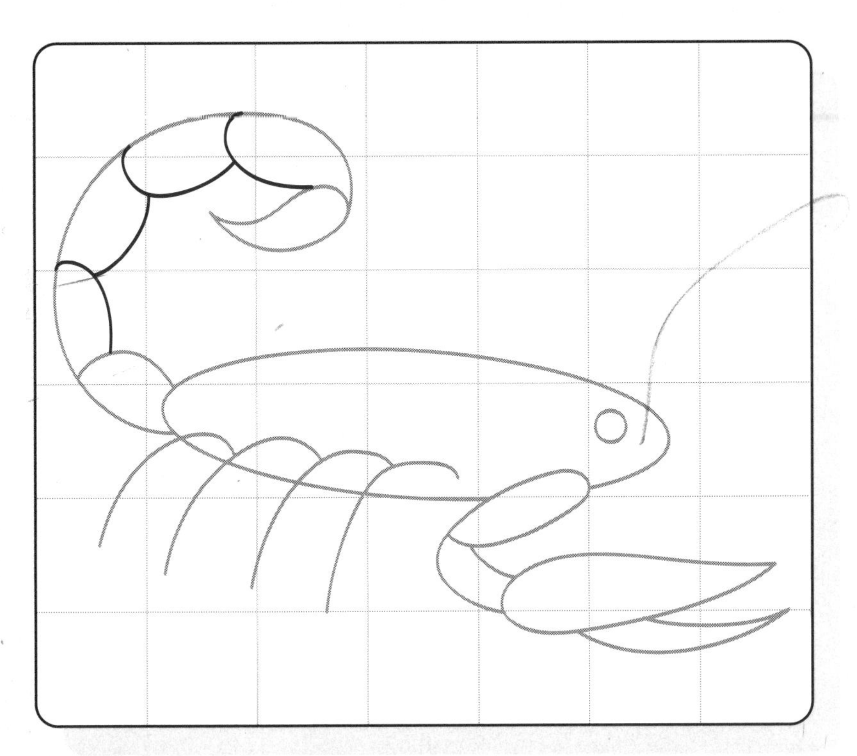

Step 5

Step 6

Step 7

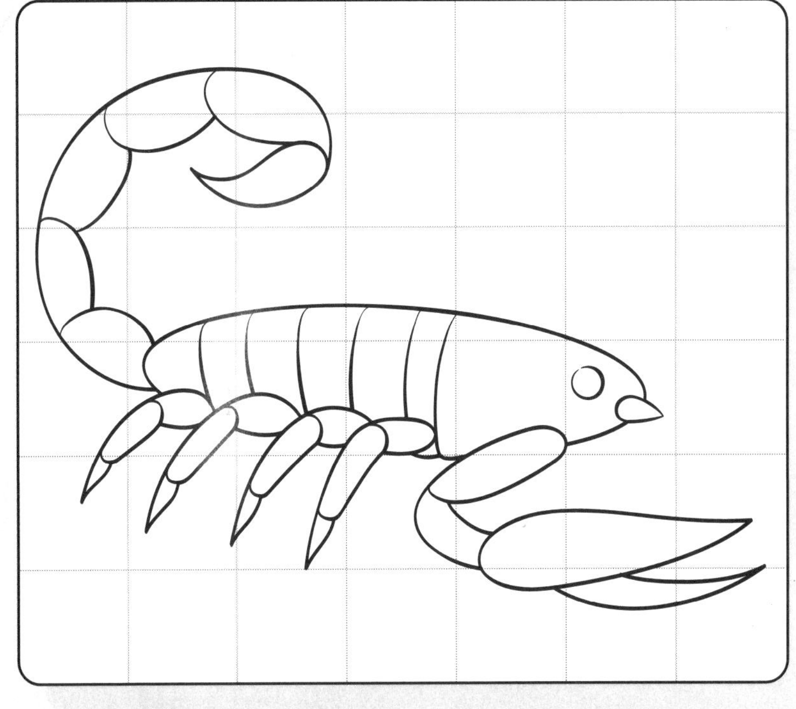

Step 8

Snail

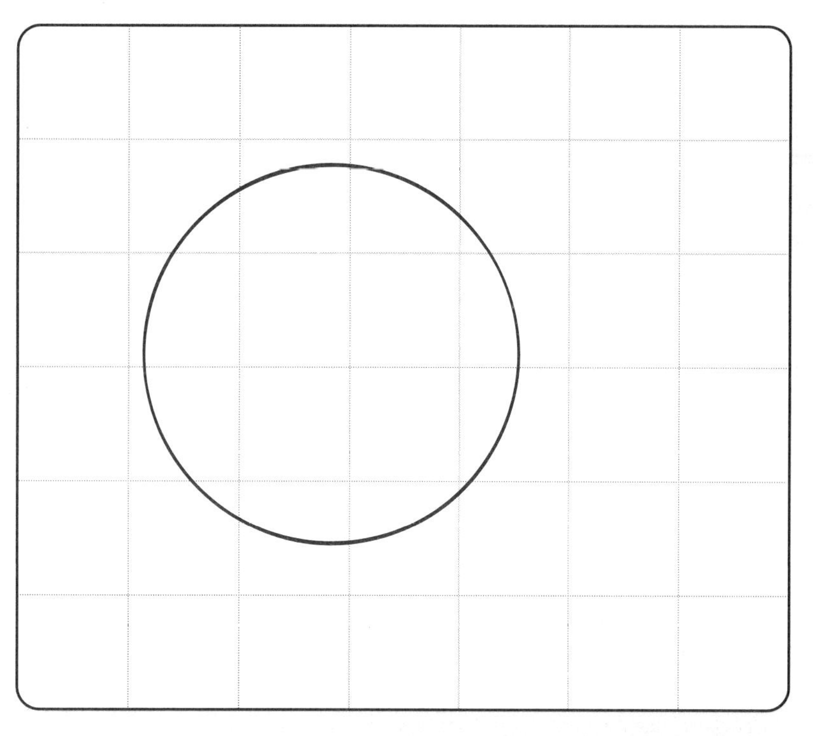

Step 1

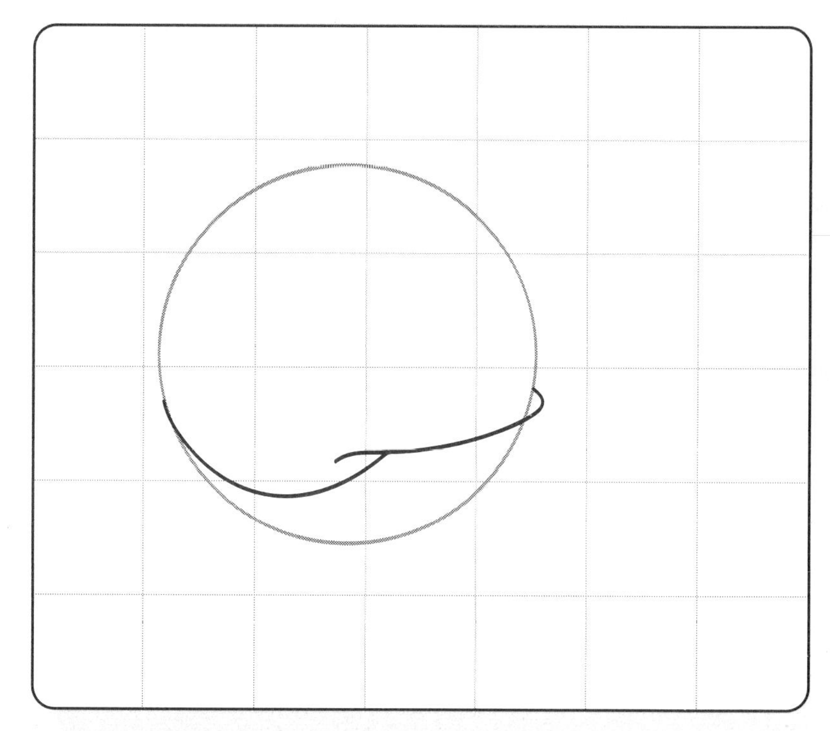

Step 2

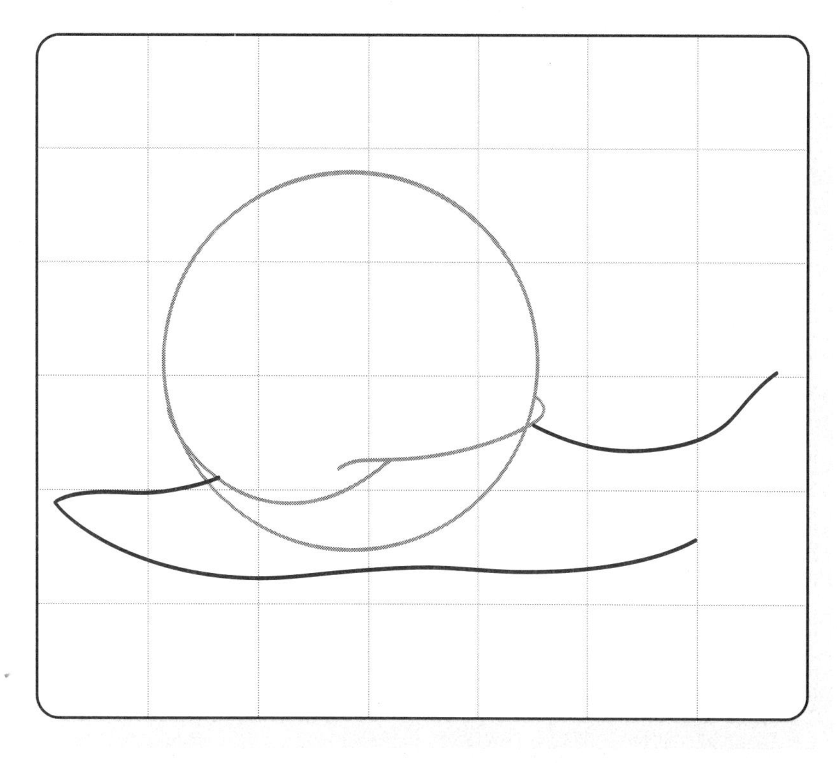

Step 3

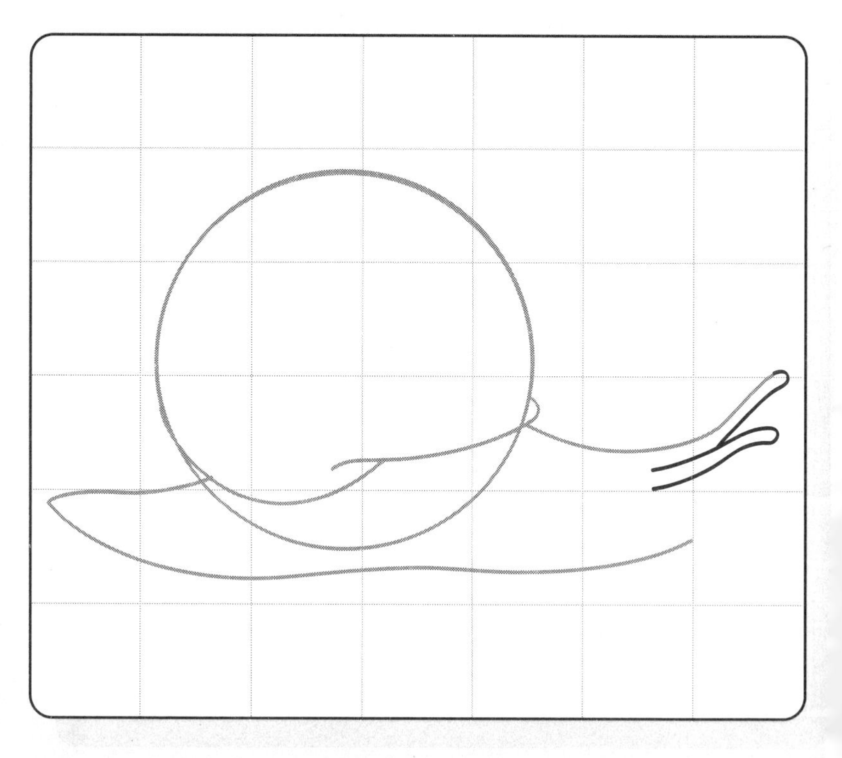

Step 4

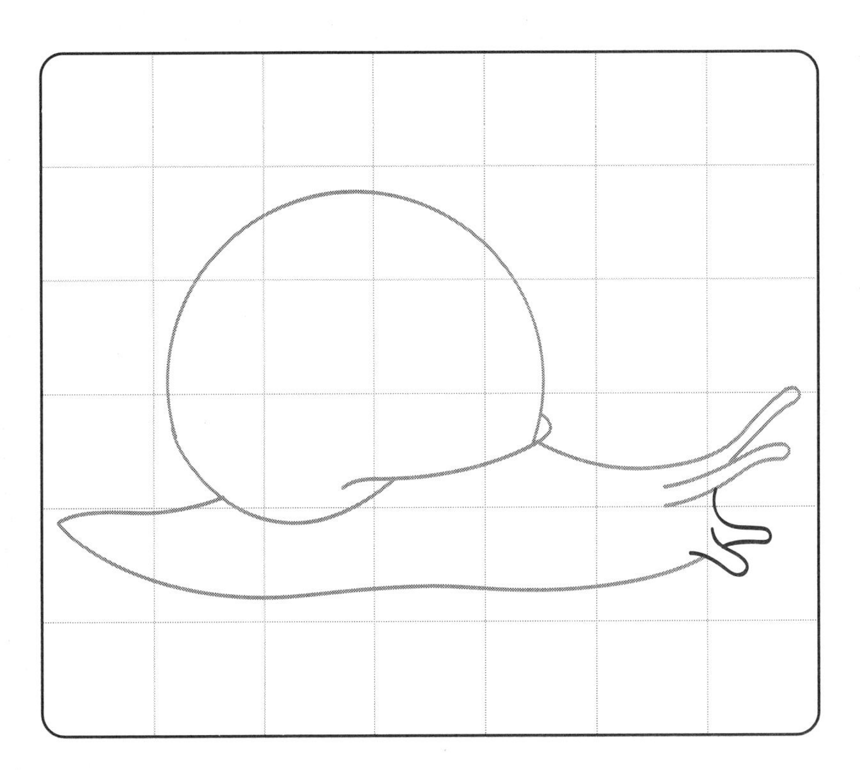

Step 5

Step 6

Step 7

Step 8

Earthworm

Step 1

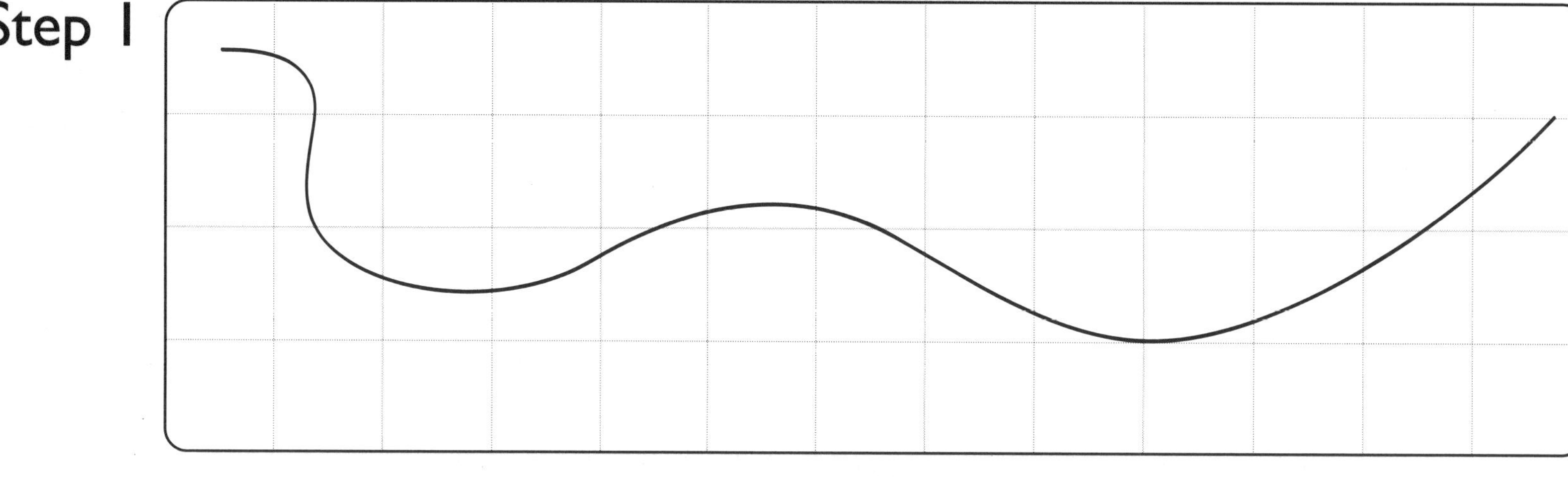

Step 2

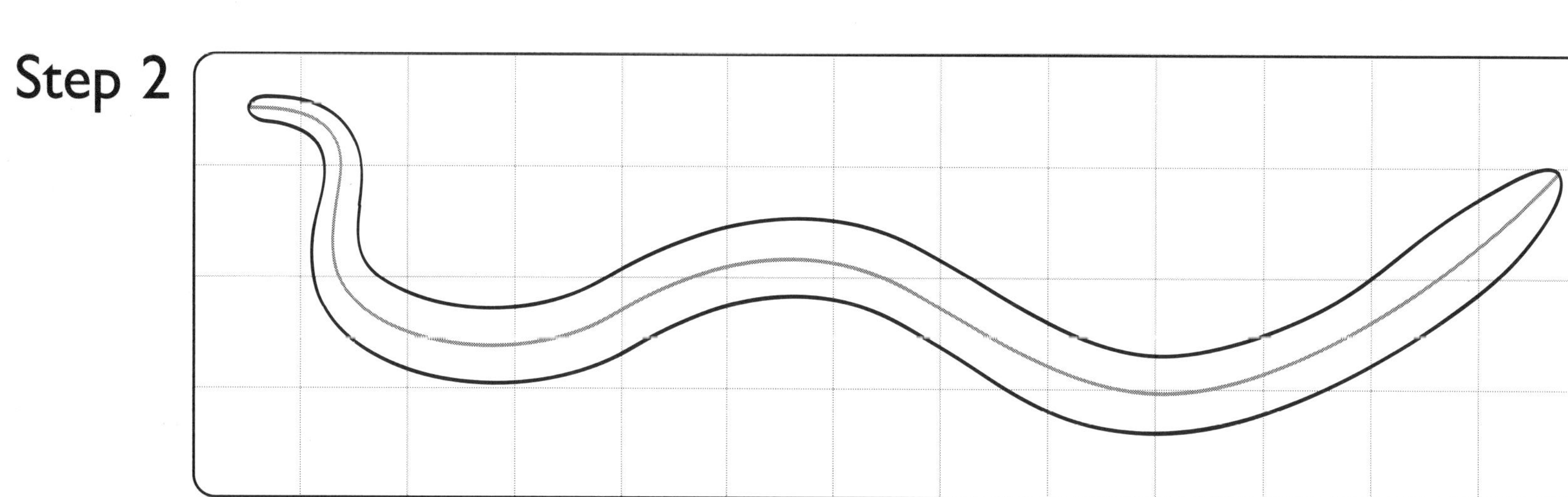

Step 3

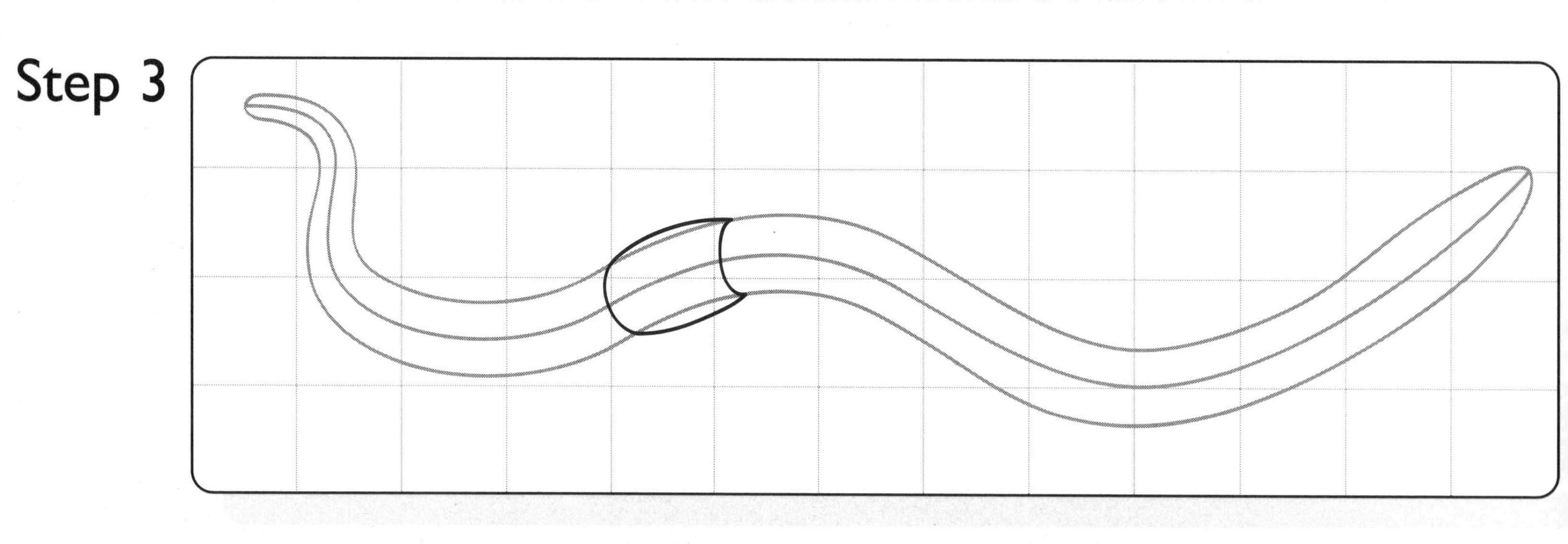

Step 4

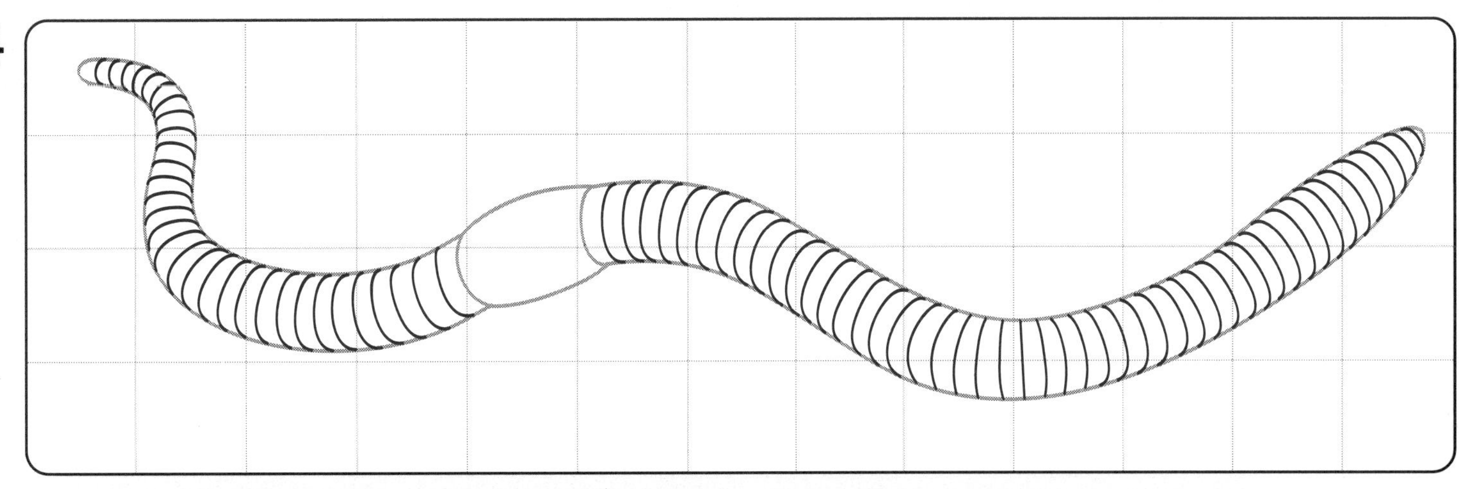

Step 5

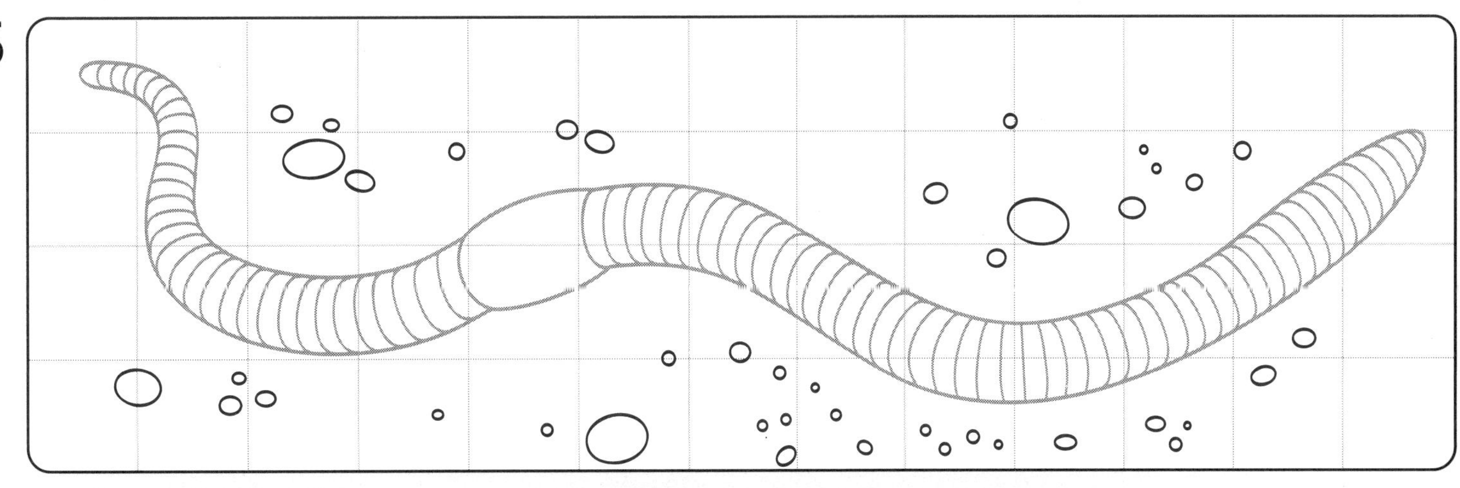

Step 6

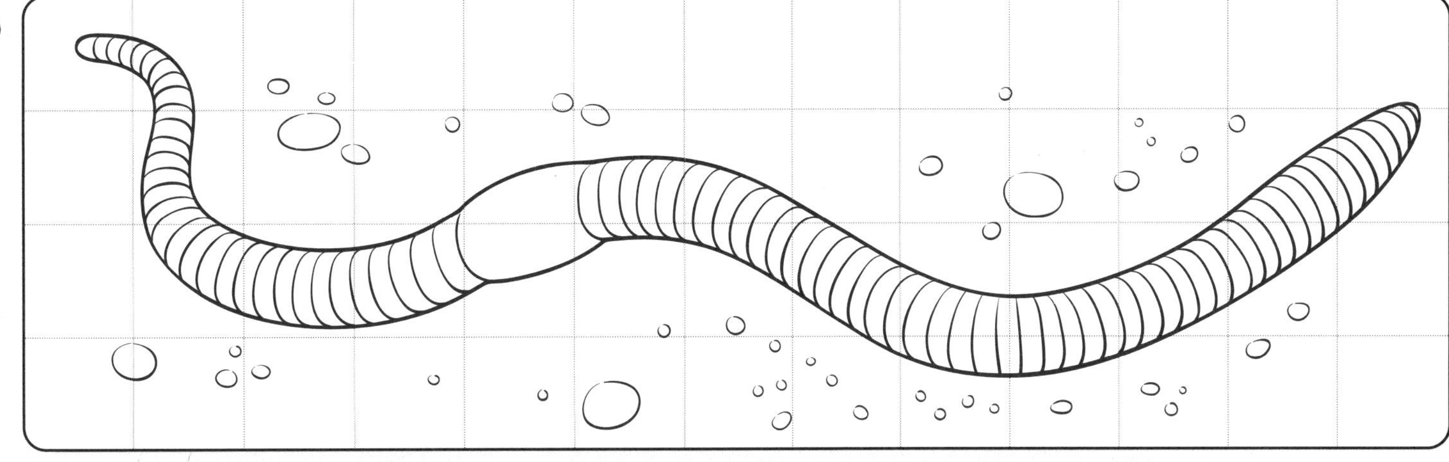

Ant

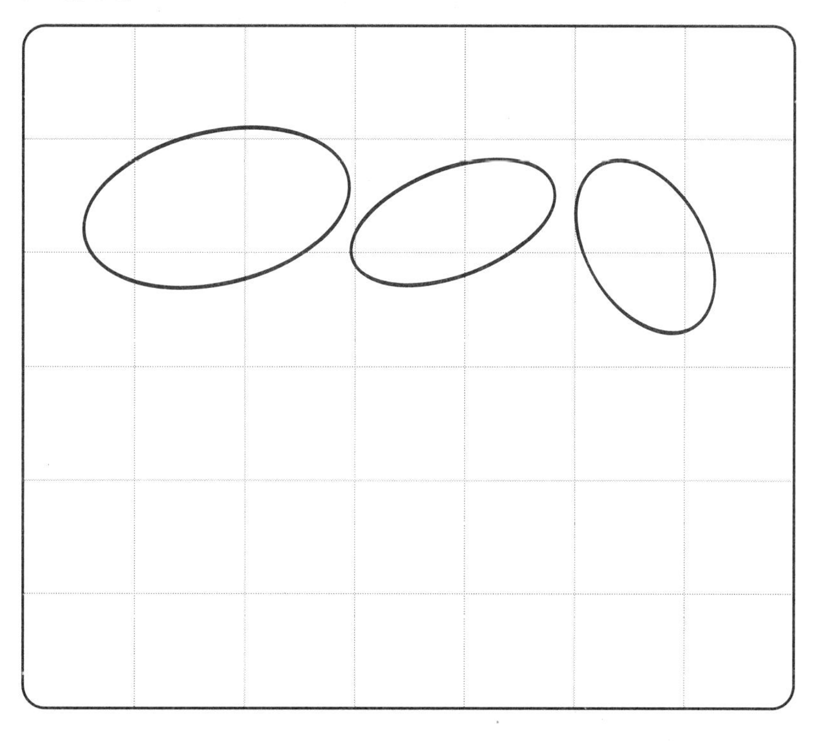

Step 1

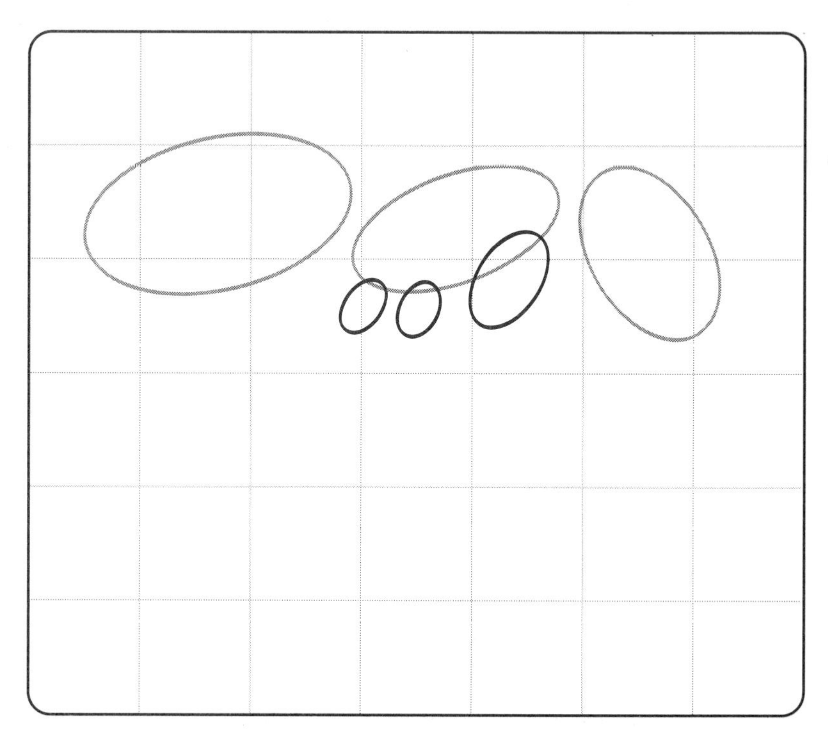

Step 2

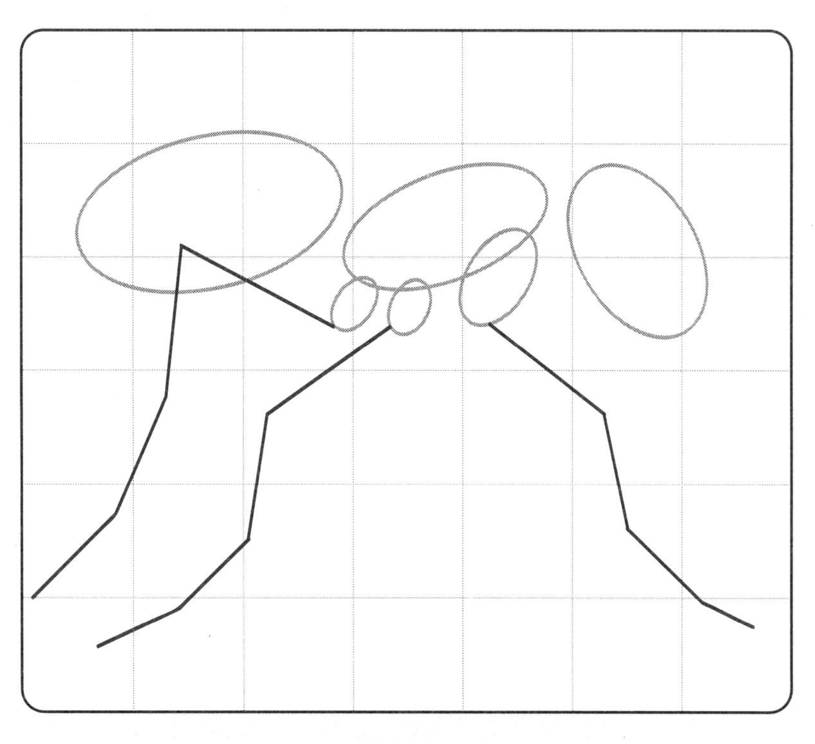

Step 3

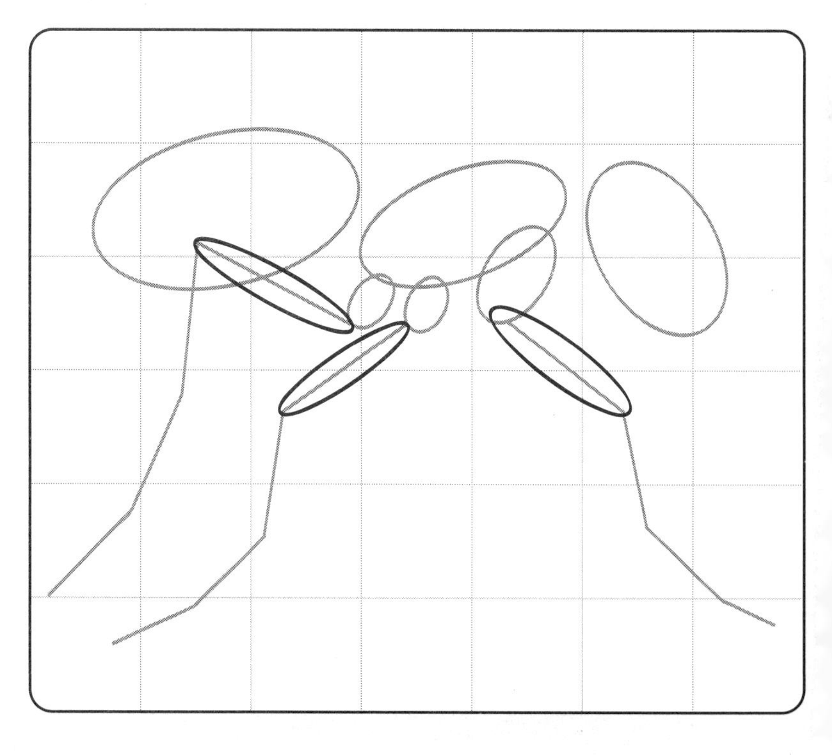

Step 4

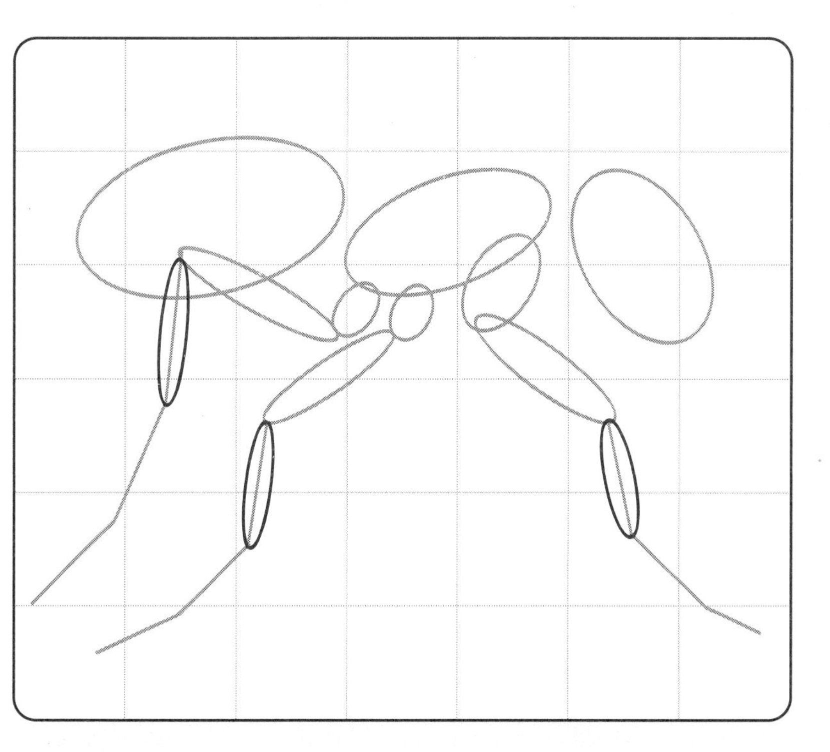

Step 5

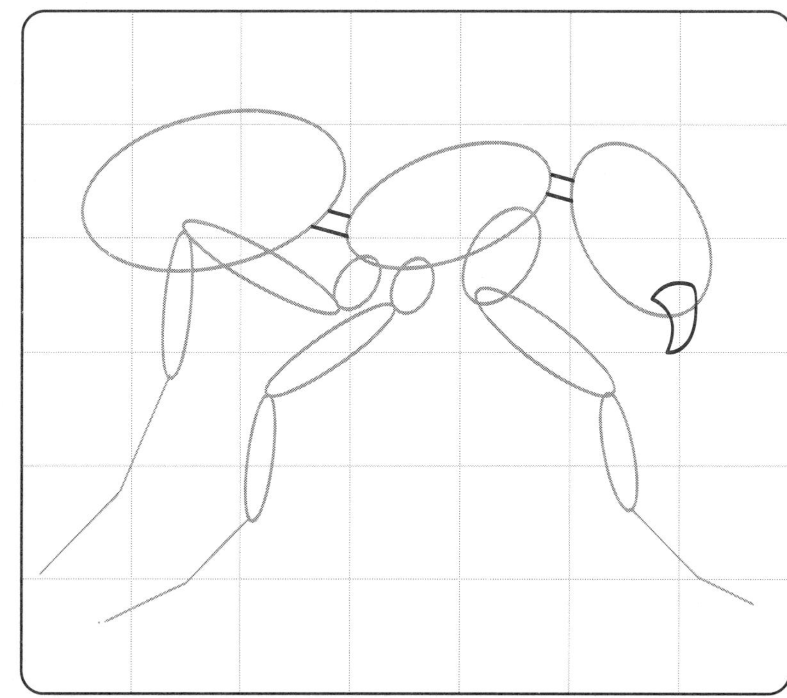

Step 6

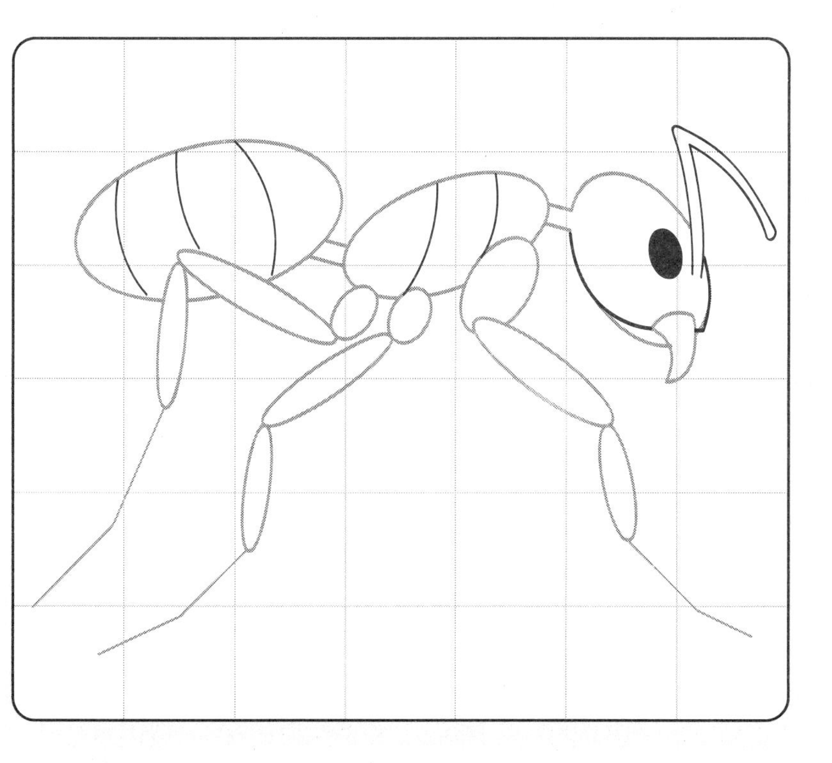

Step 7

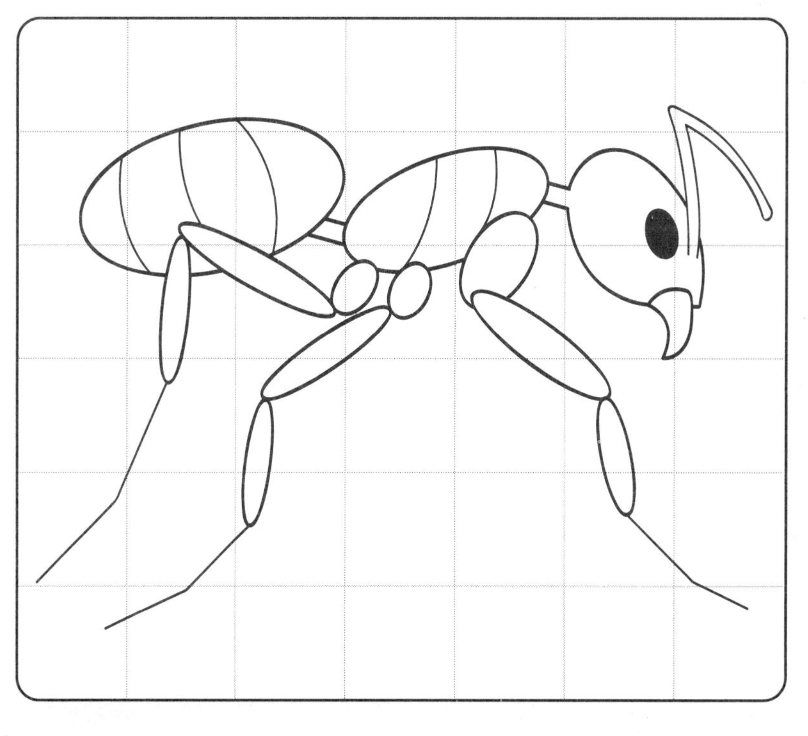

Step 8

Earwig

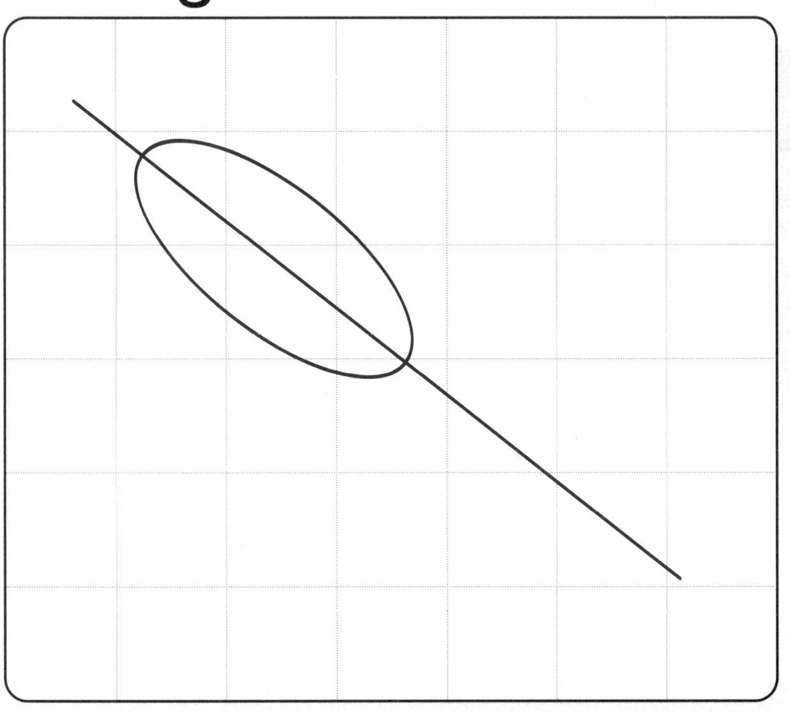

Step 1

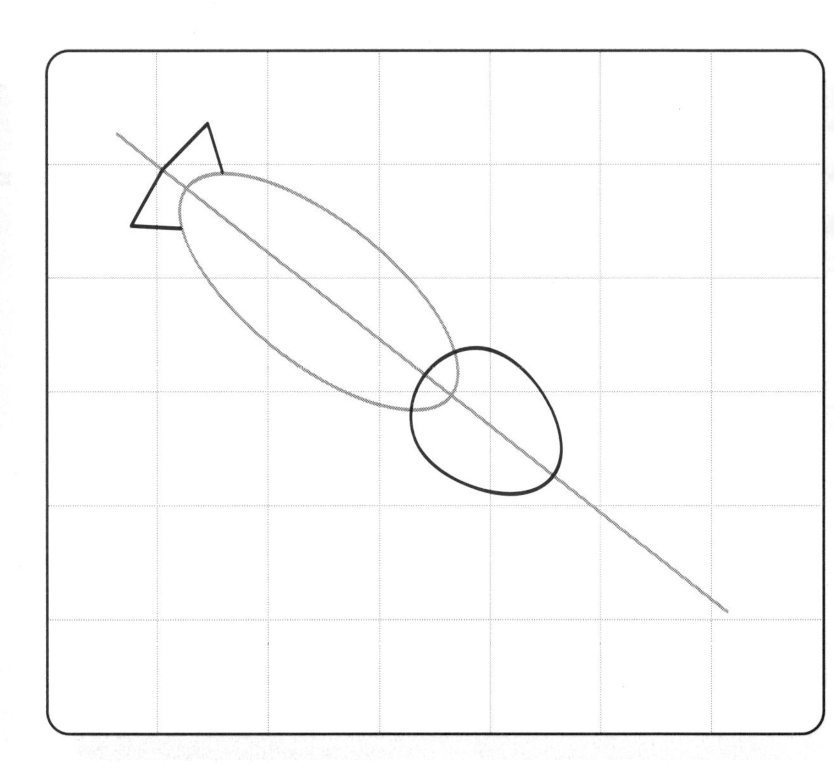

Step 2

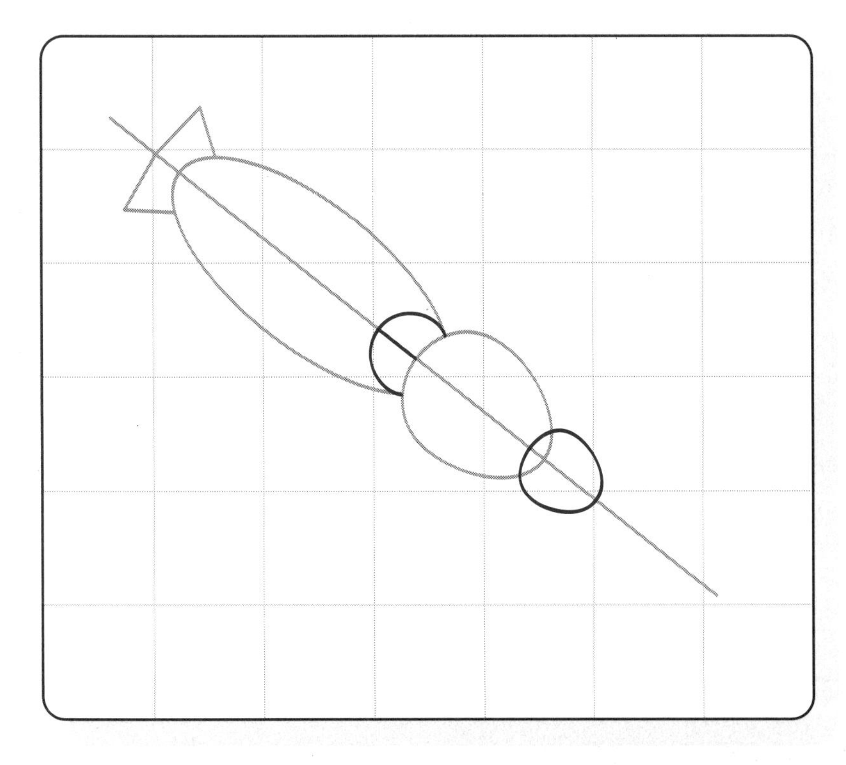

Step 3

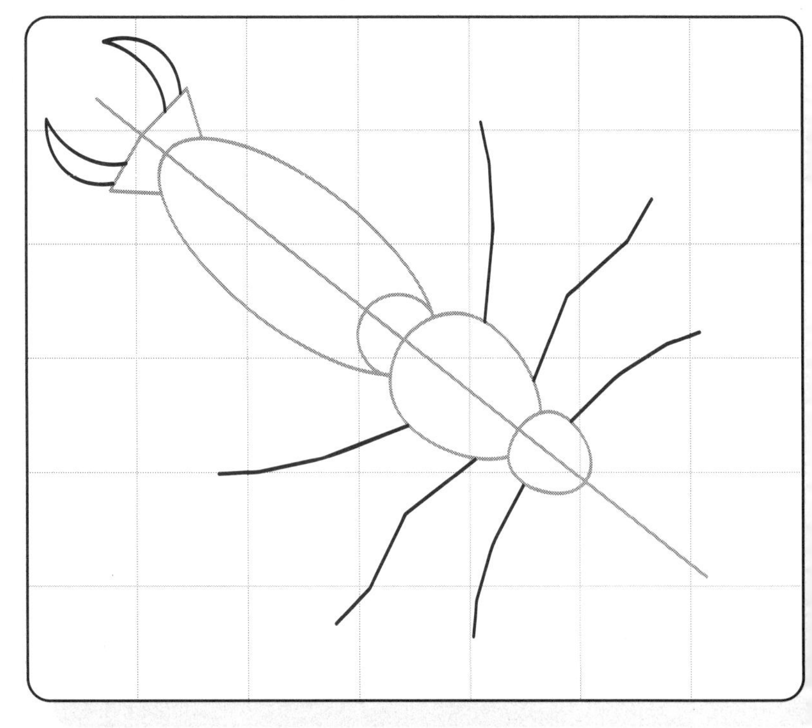

Step 4

Step 5

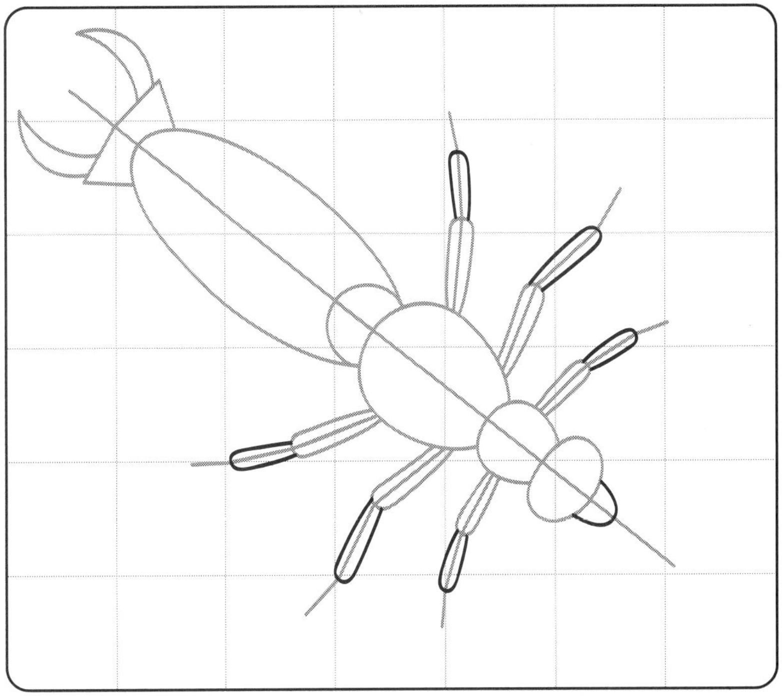

Step 6

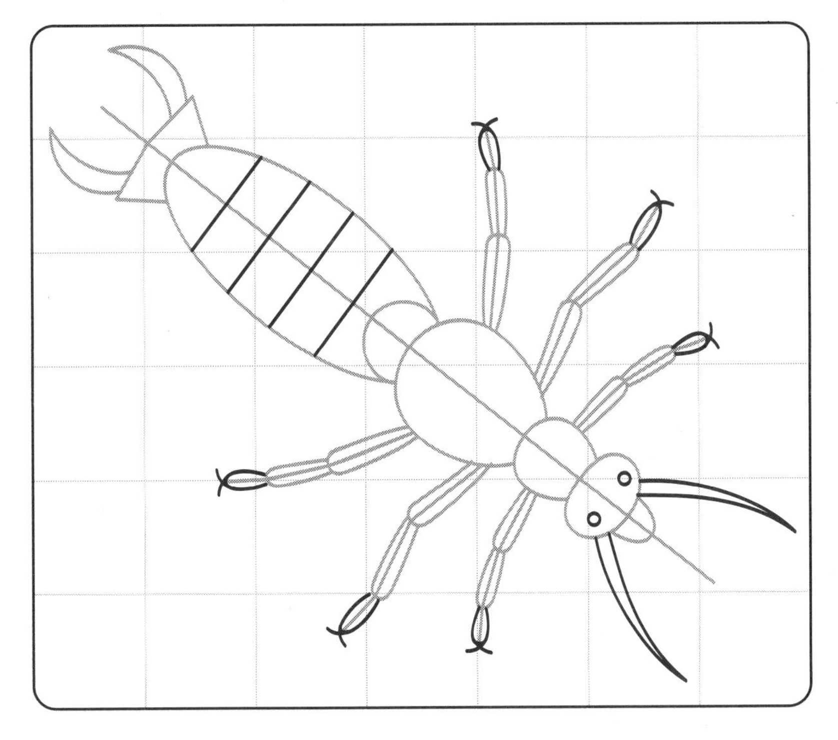

Step 7

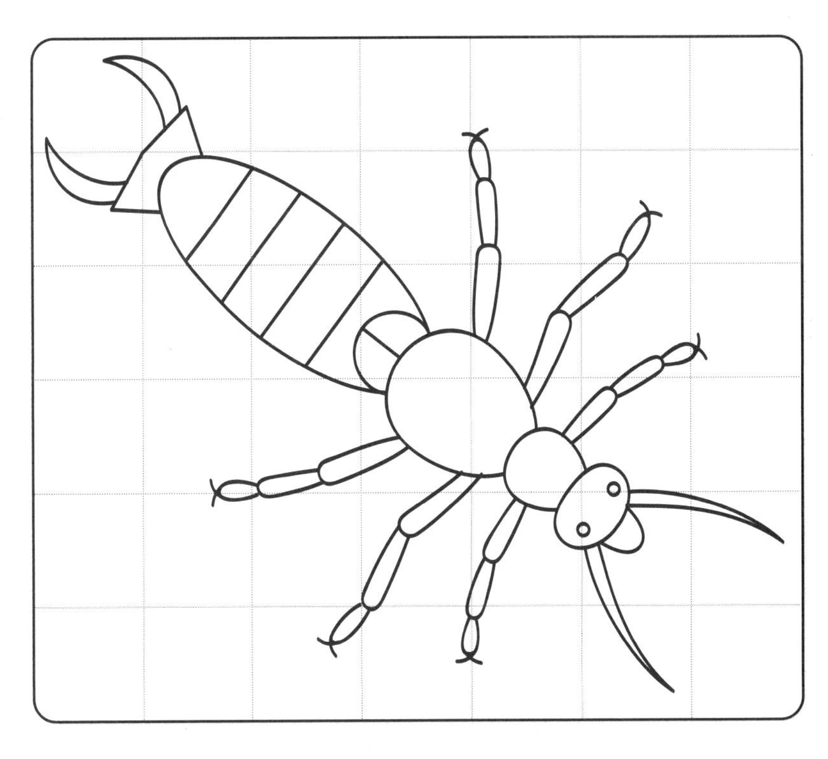

Step 8

Spider

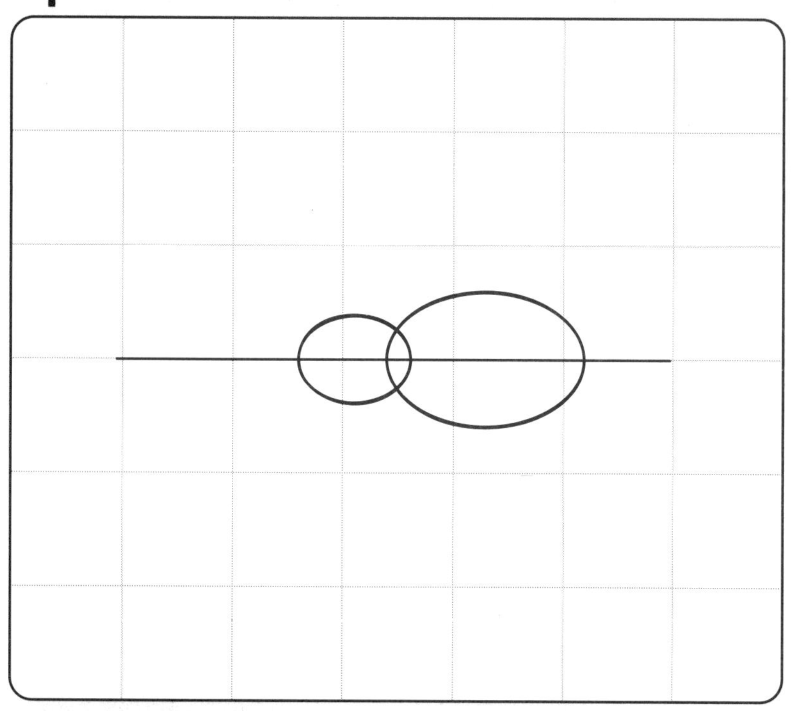

Step 1

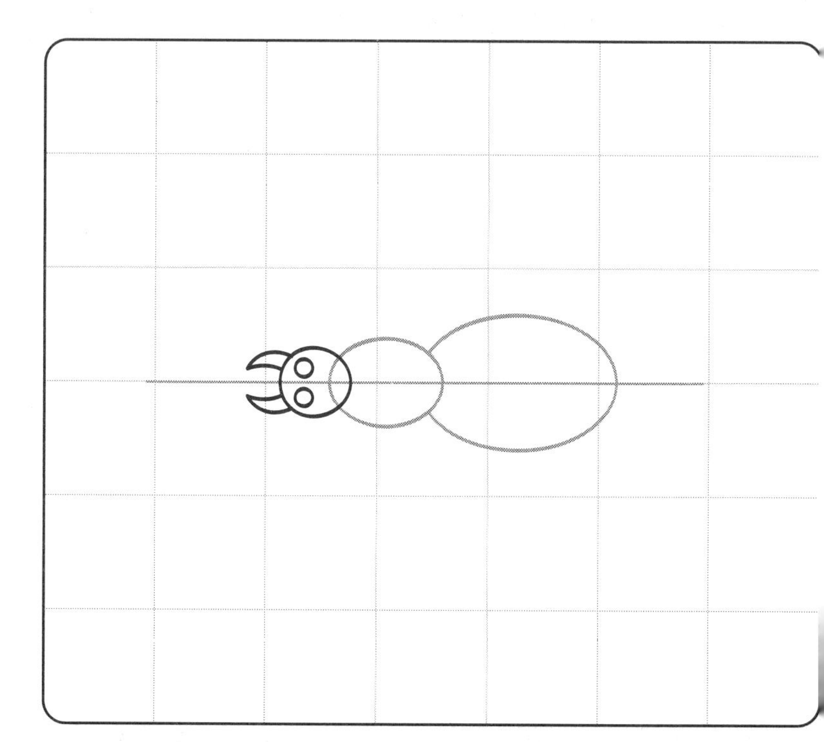

Step 2

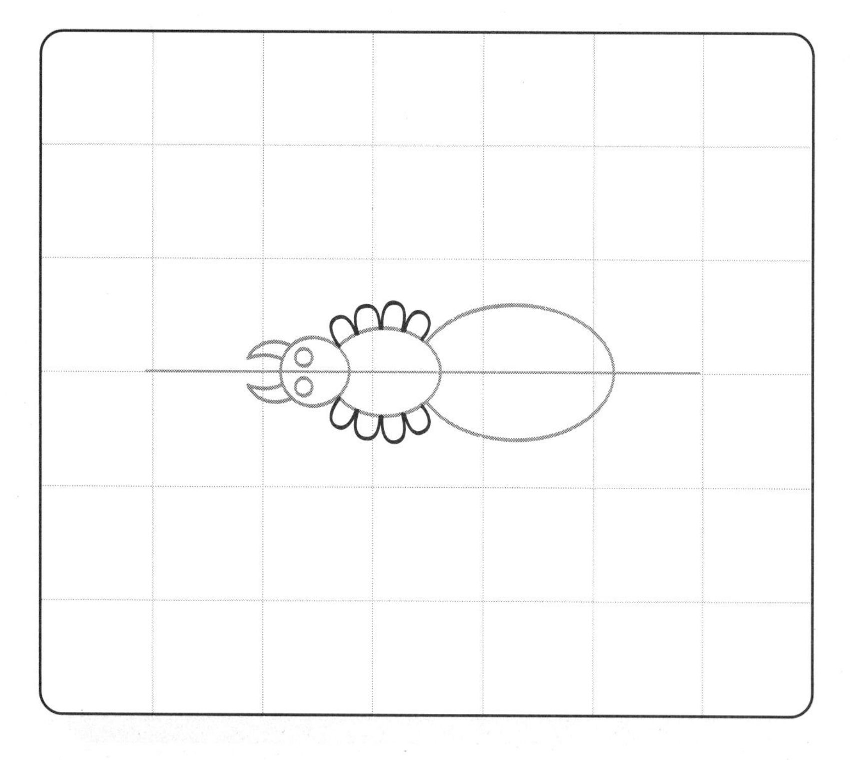

Step 3

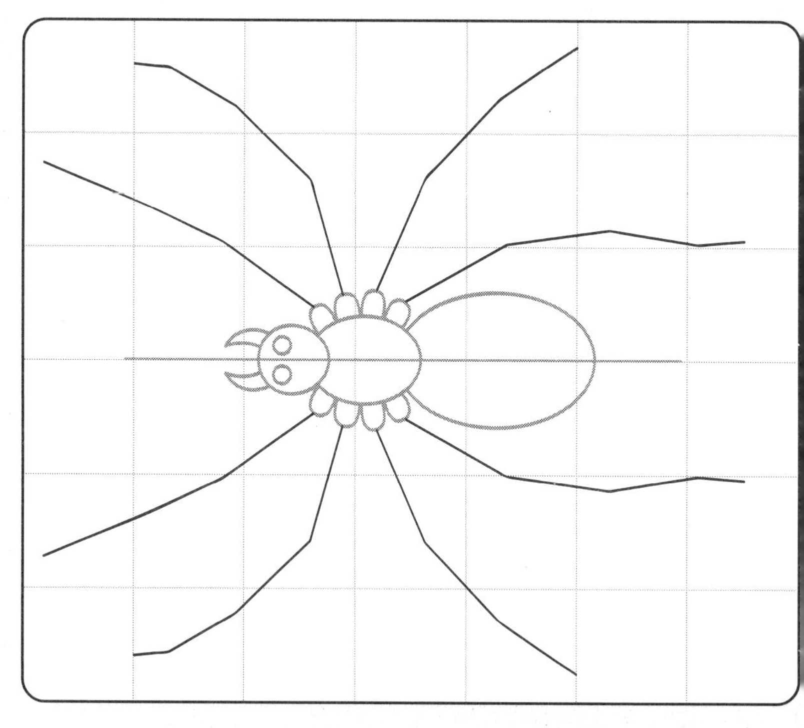

Step 4

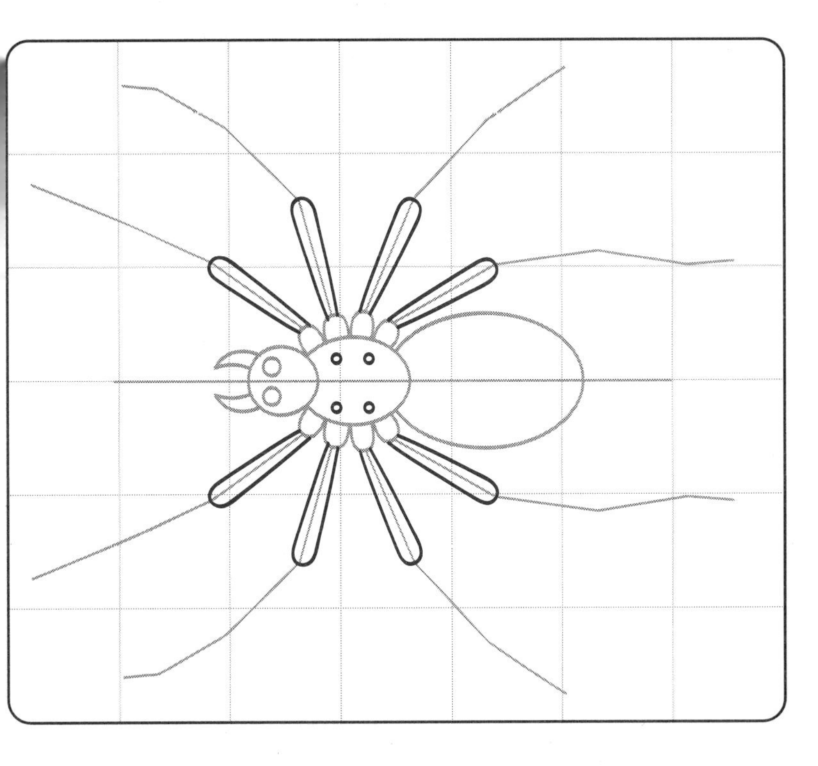

Step 5

Step 6

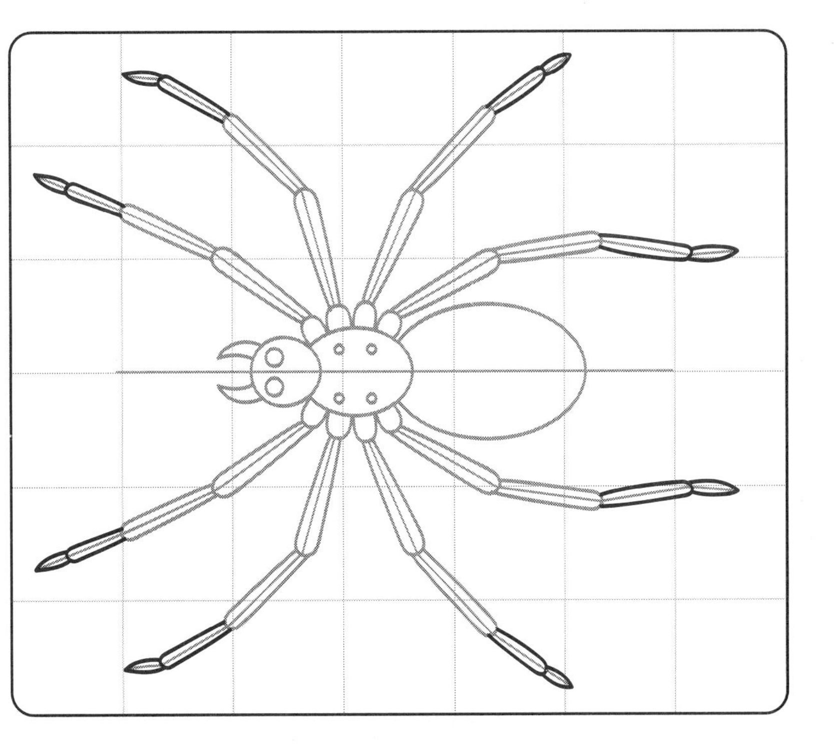

Step 7

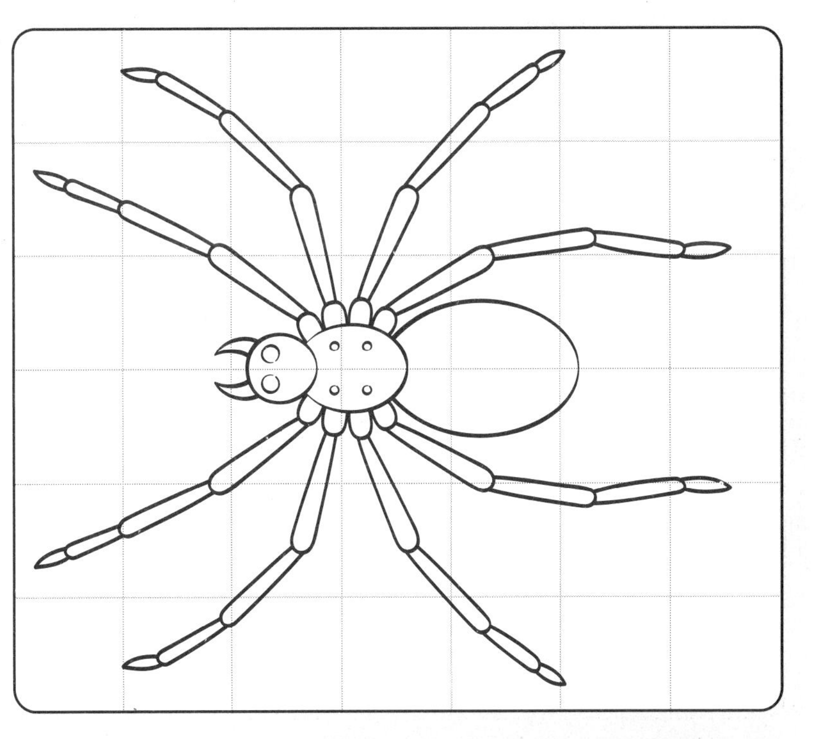

Step 8

Fly

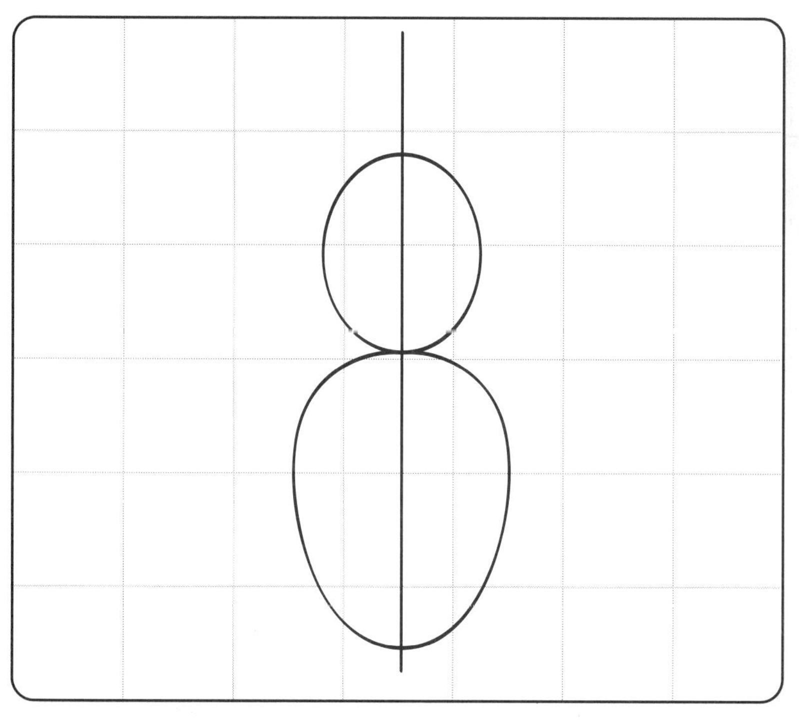

Step 1

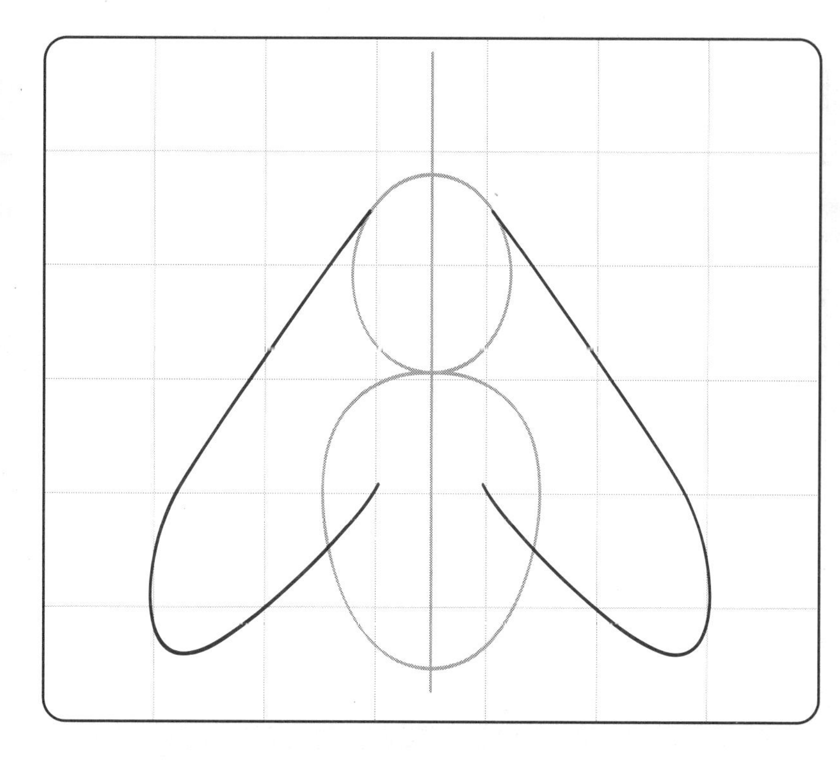

Step 2

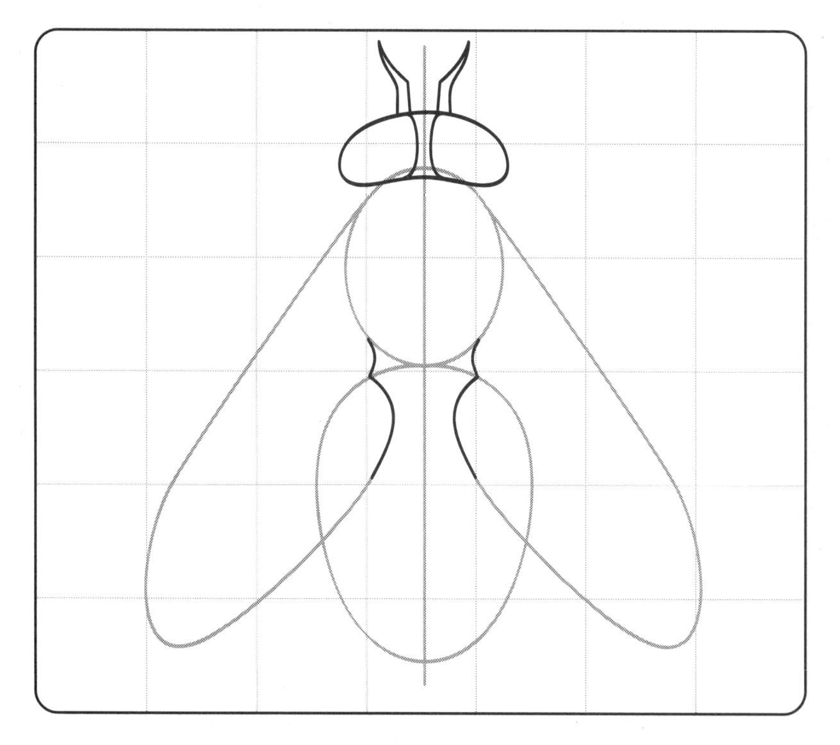

Step 3

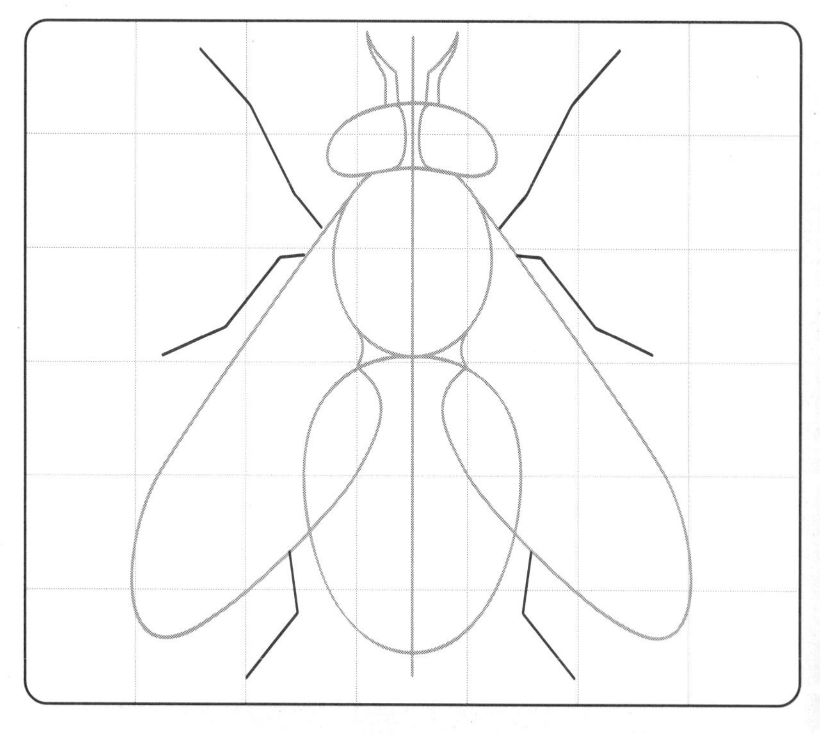

Step 4

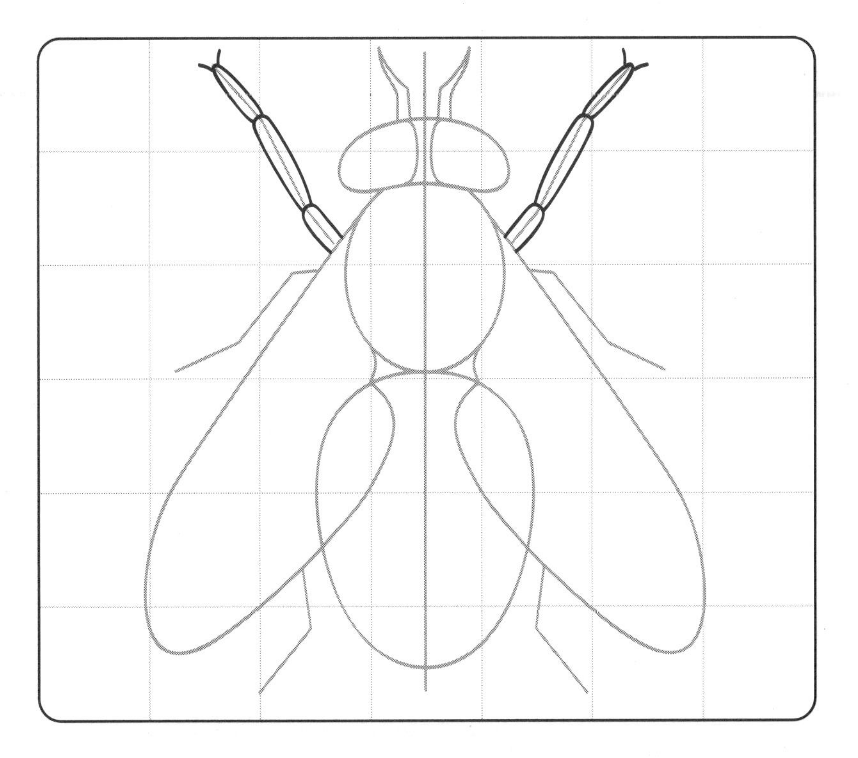

Step 5

Step 6

Step 7

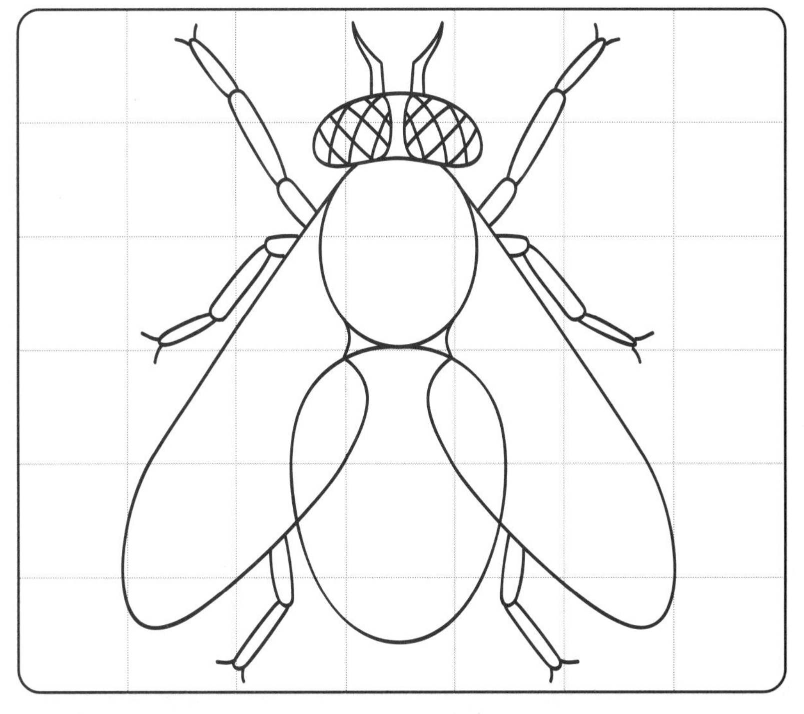

Step 8

Ladybug

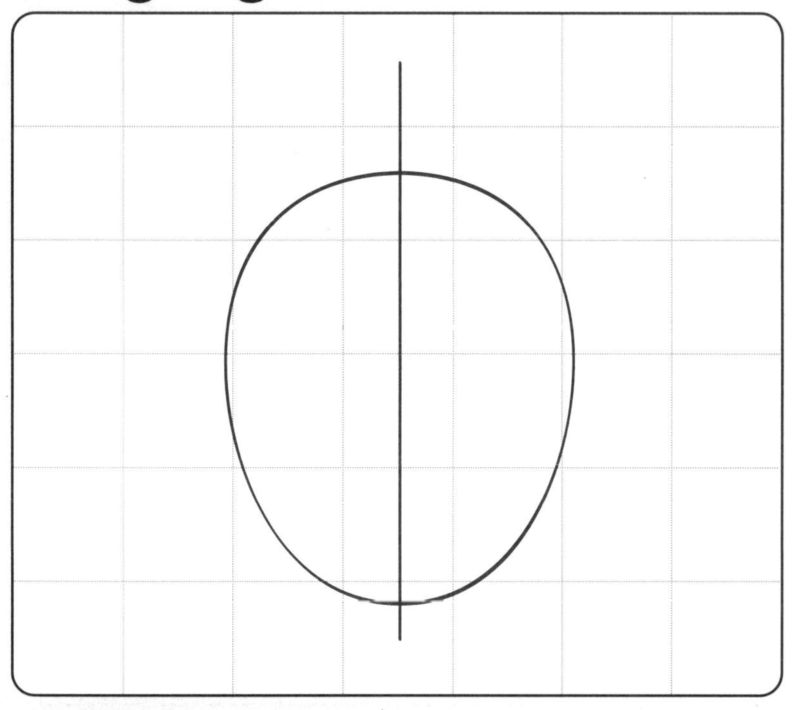

Step 1

Step 2

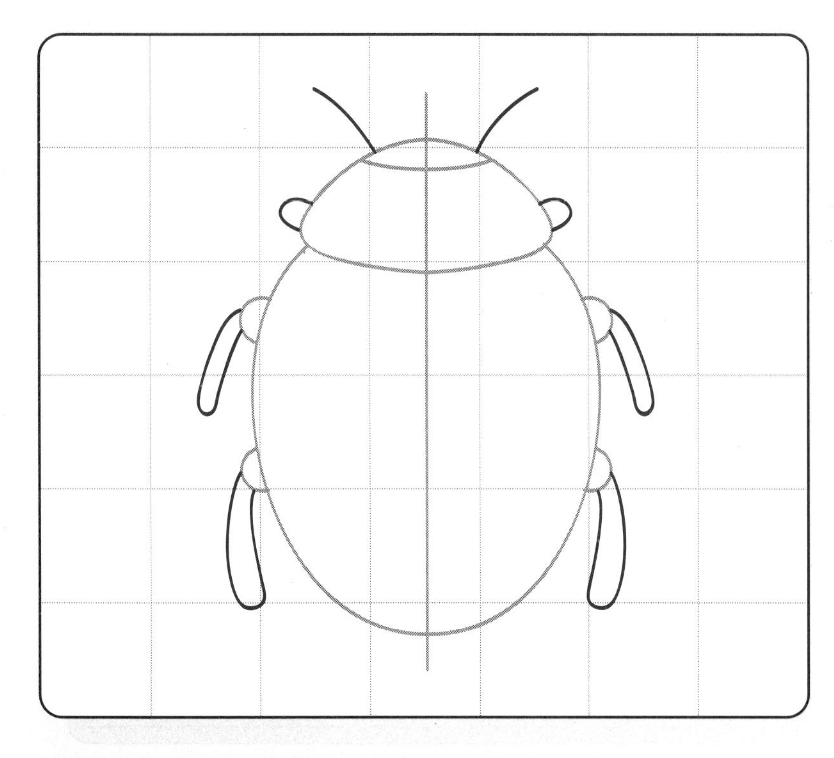

Step 3

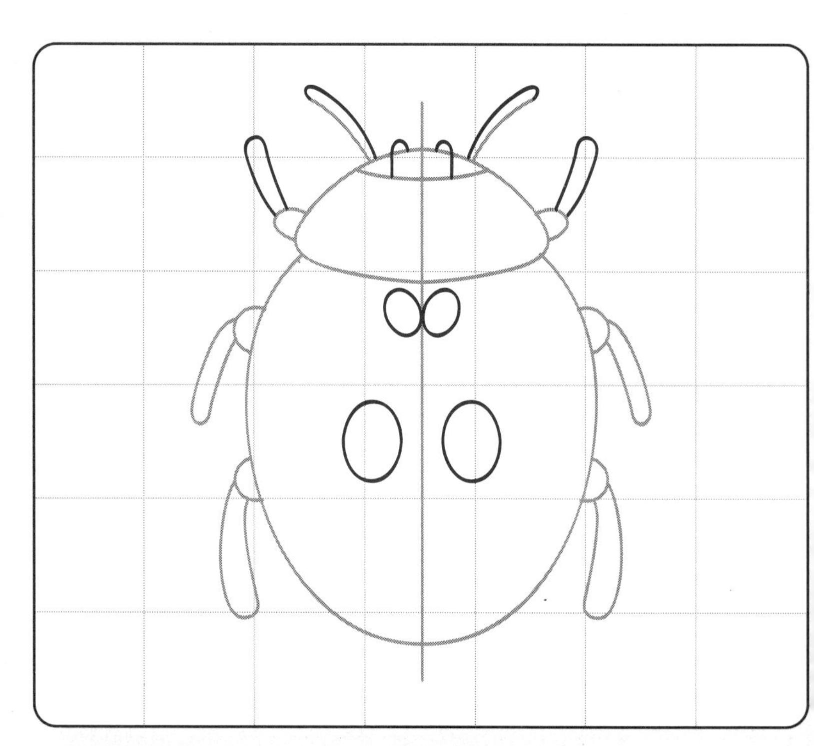

Step 4

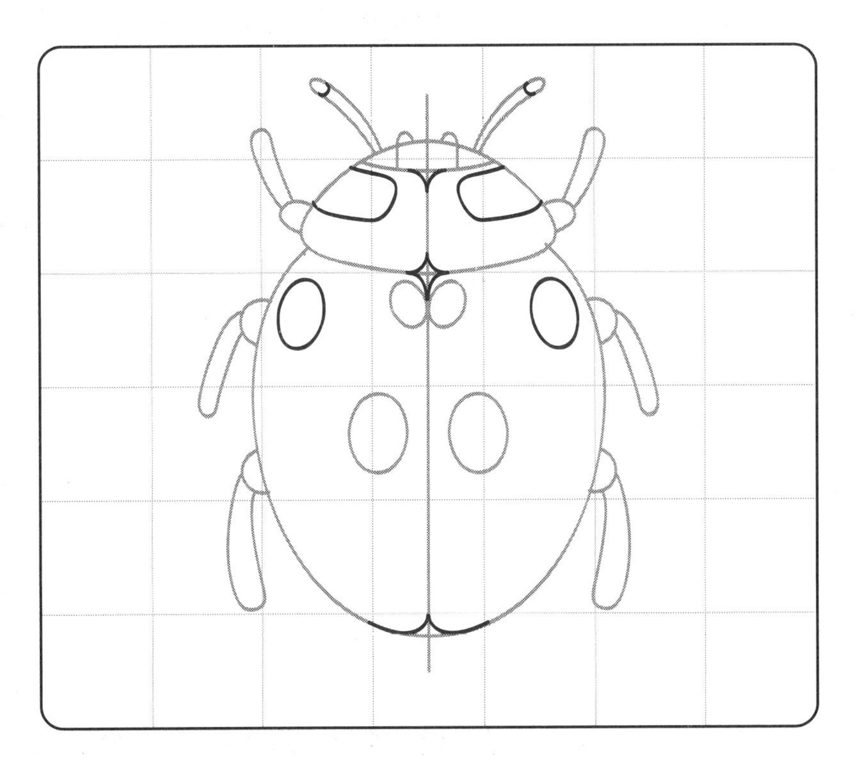

Step 5

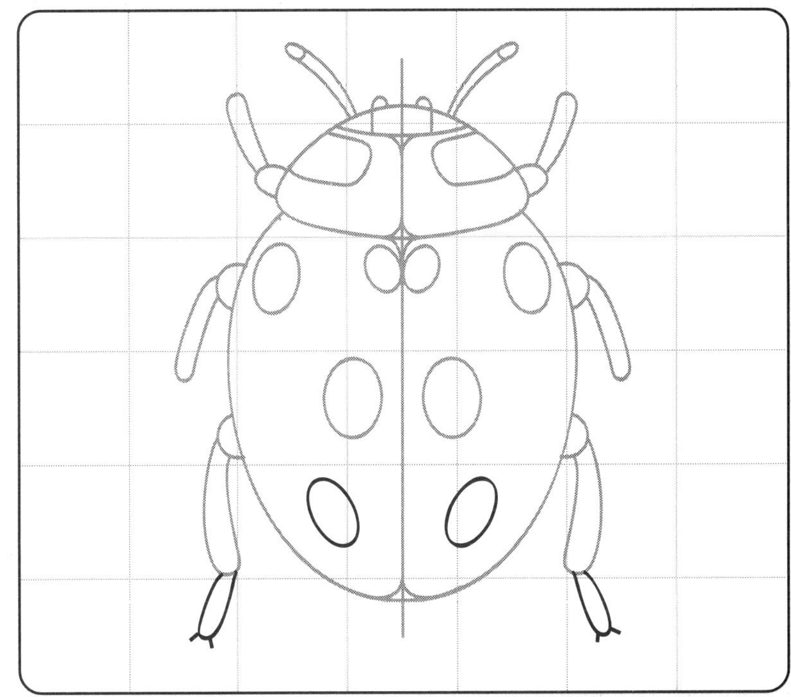

Step 6

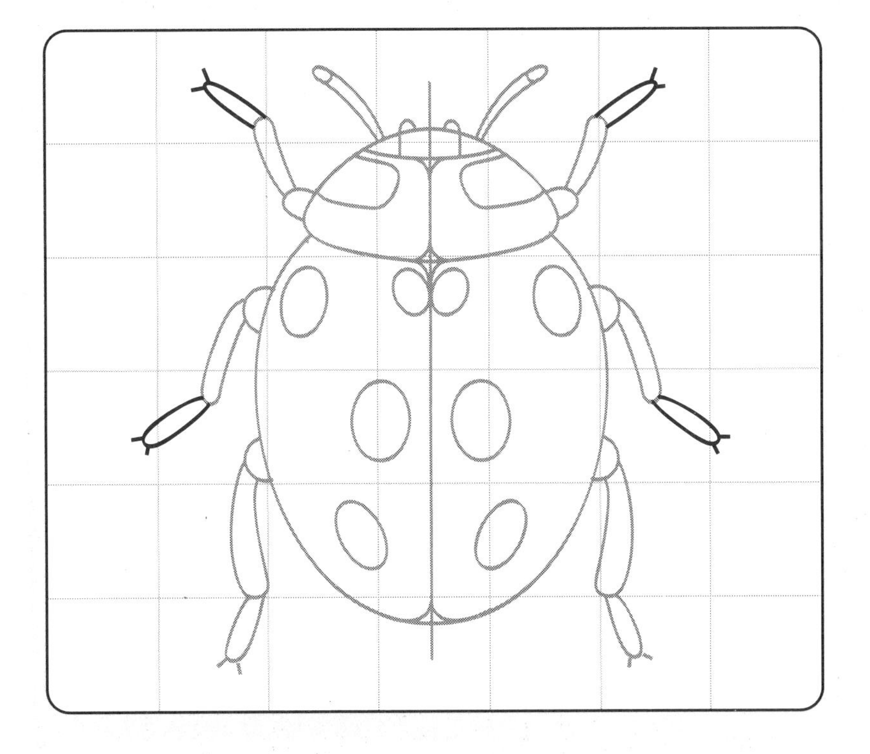

Step 7

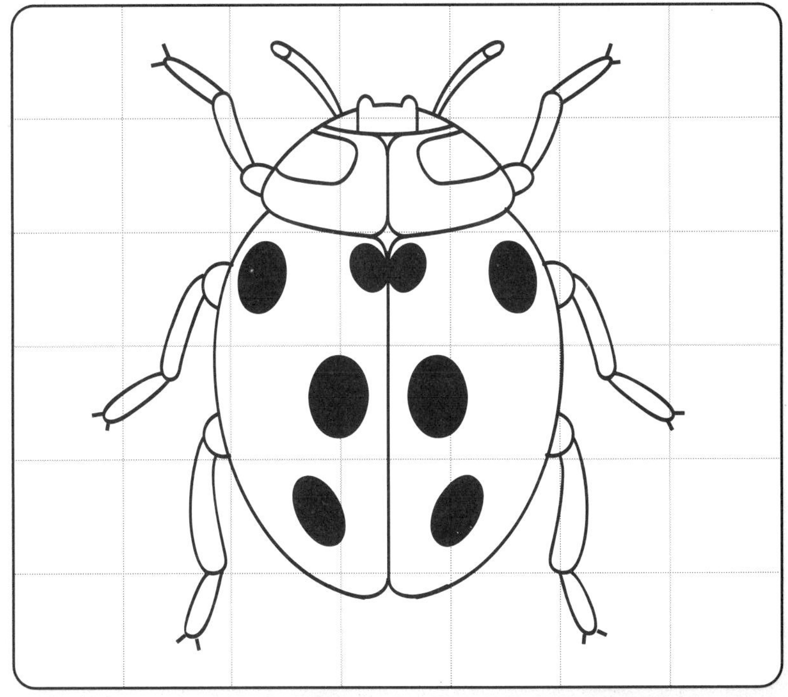

Step 8

Beetle

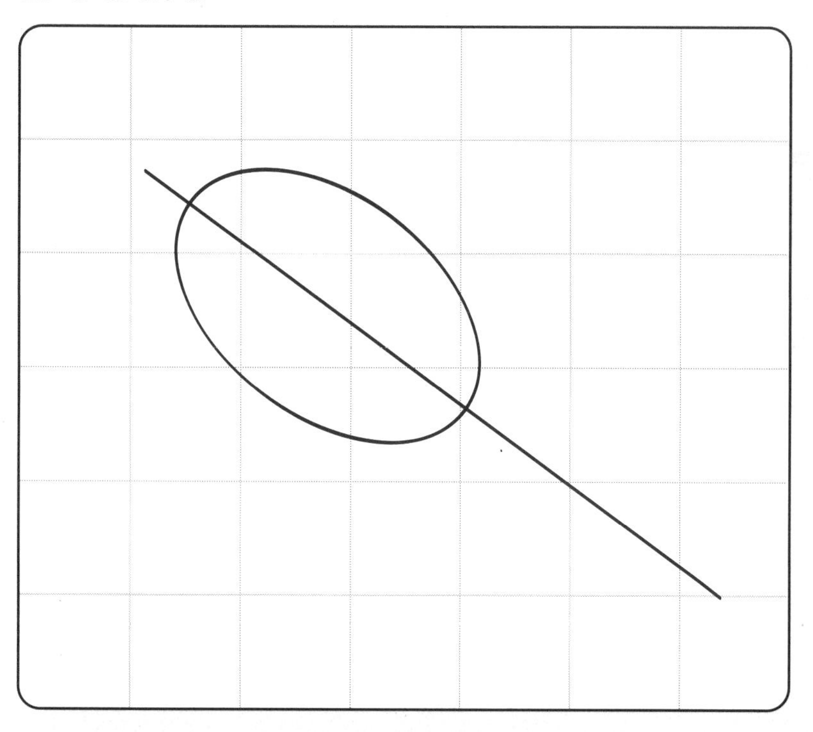

Step 1

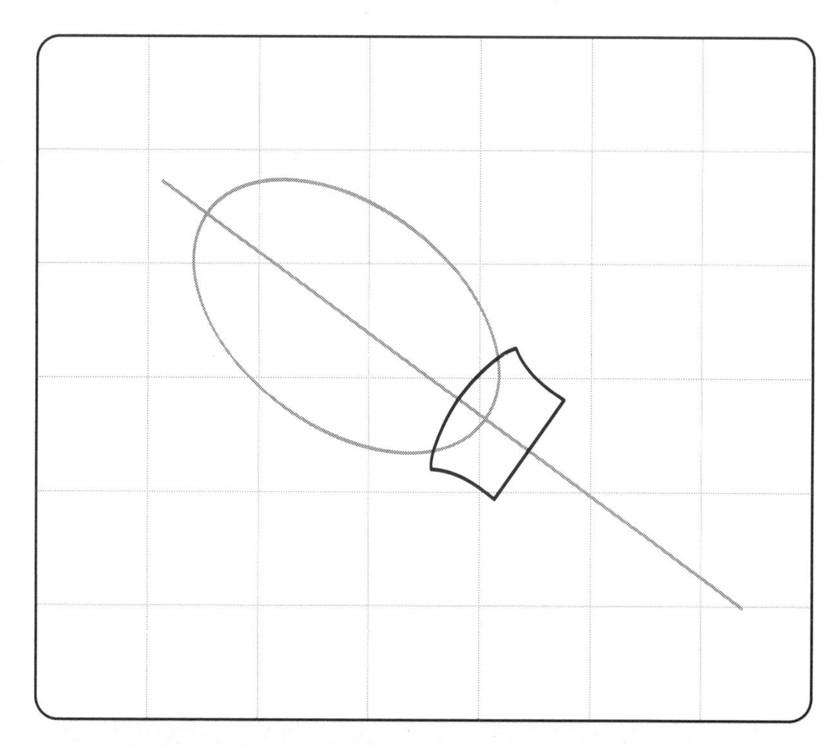

Step 2

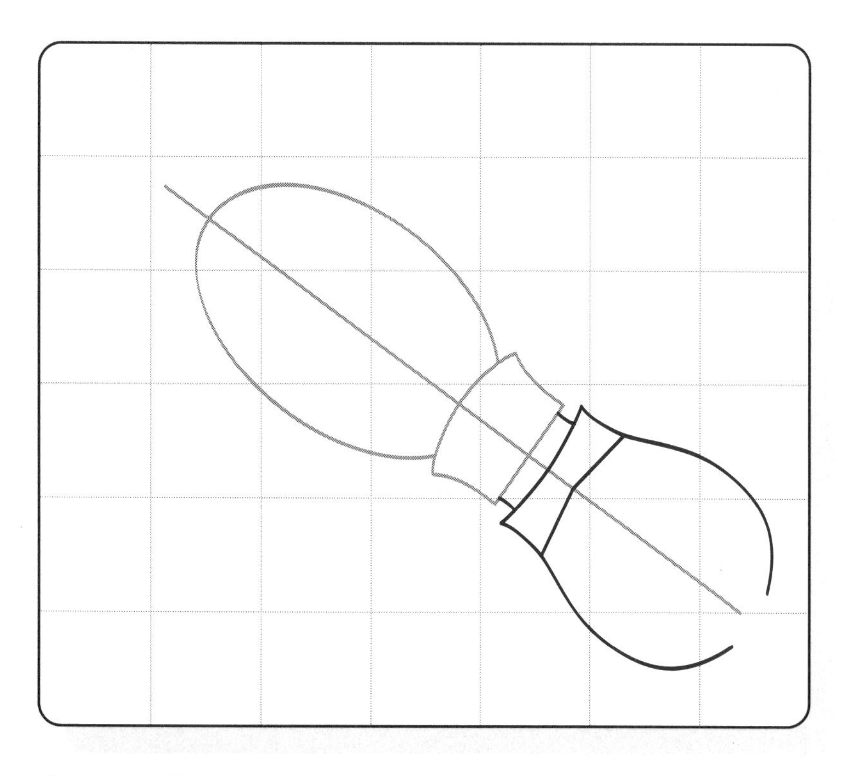

Step 3

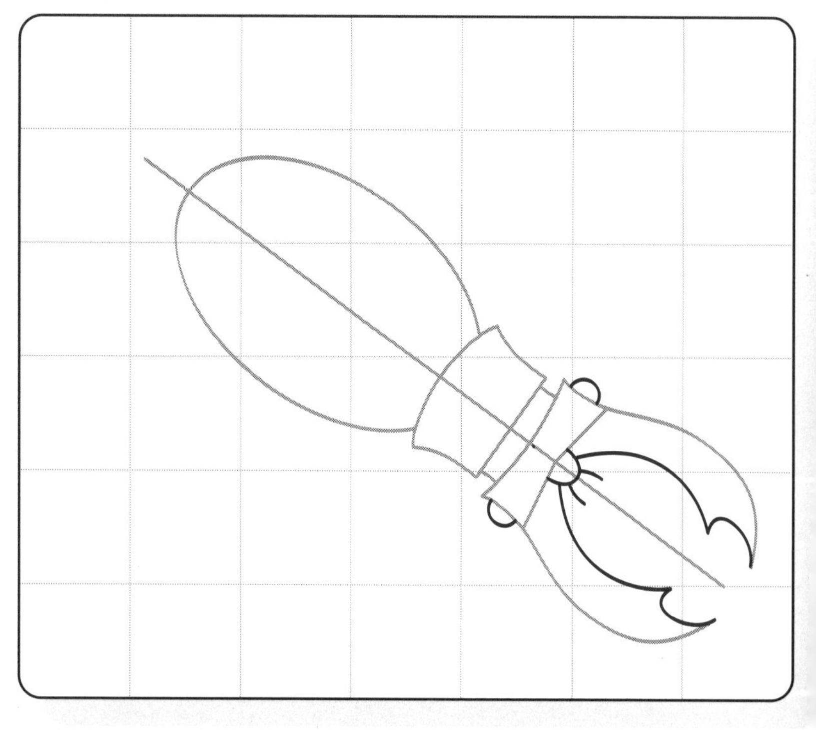

Step 4

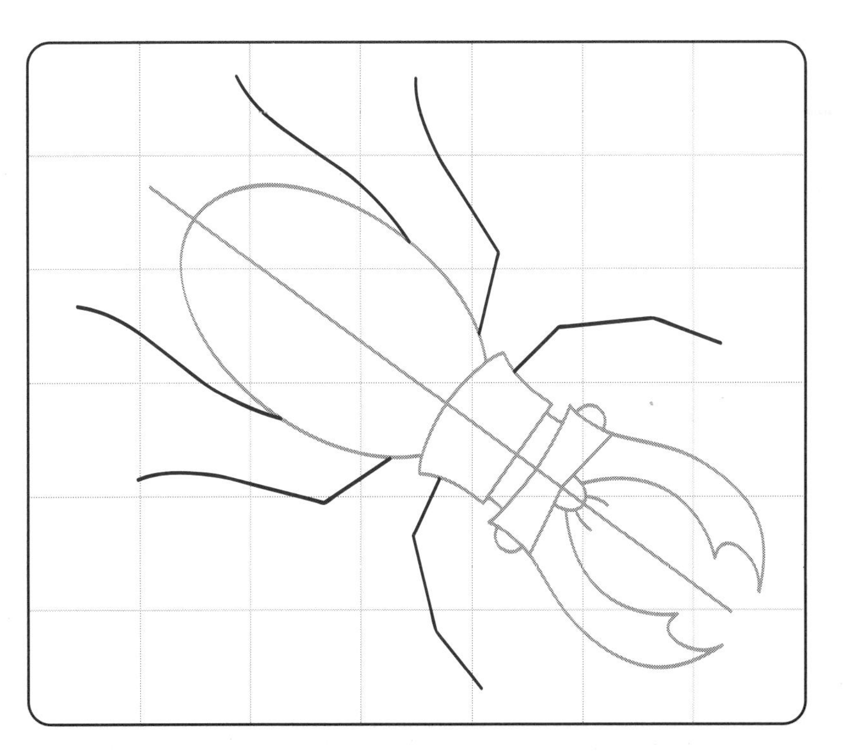

Step 5

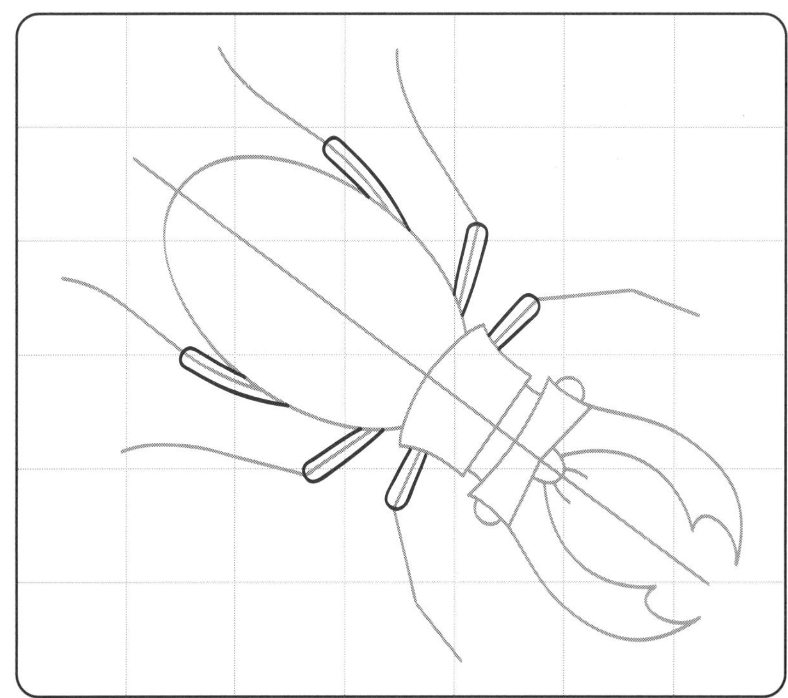

Step 6

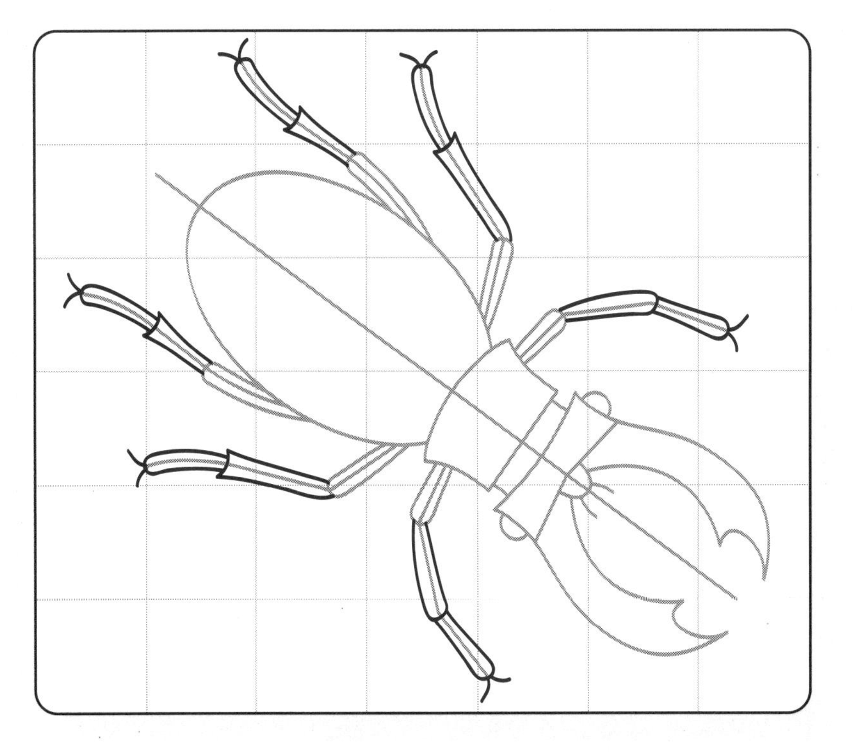

Step 7

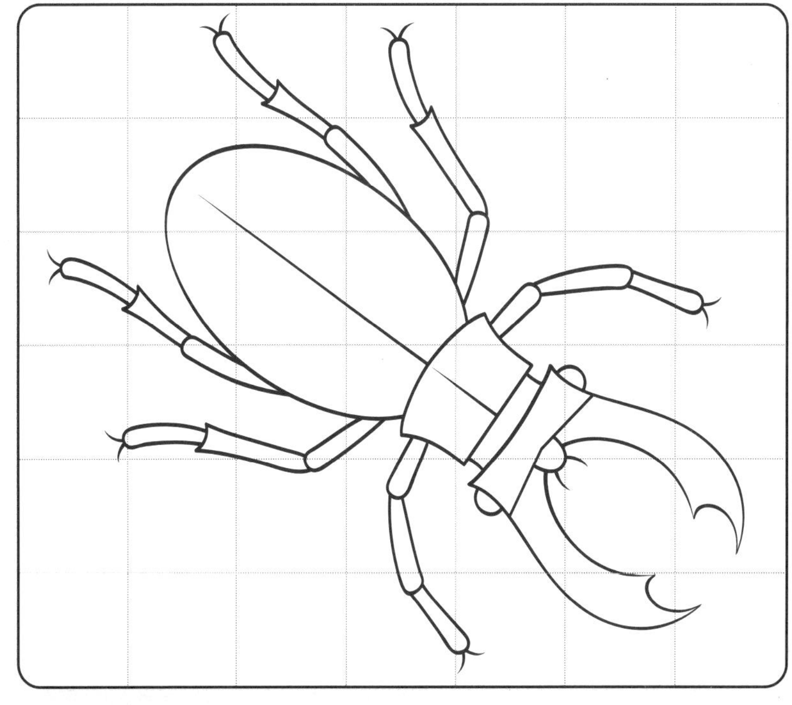

Step 8

Bumblebee

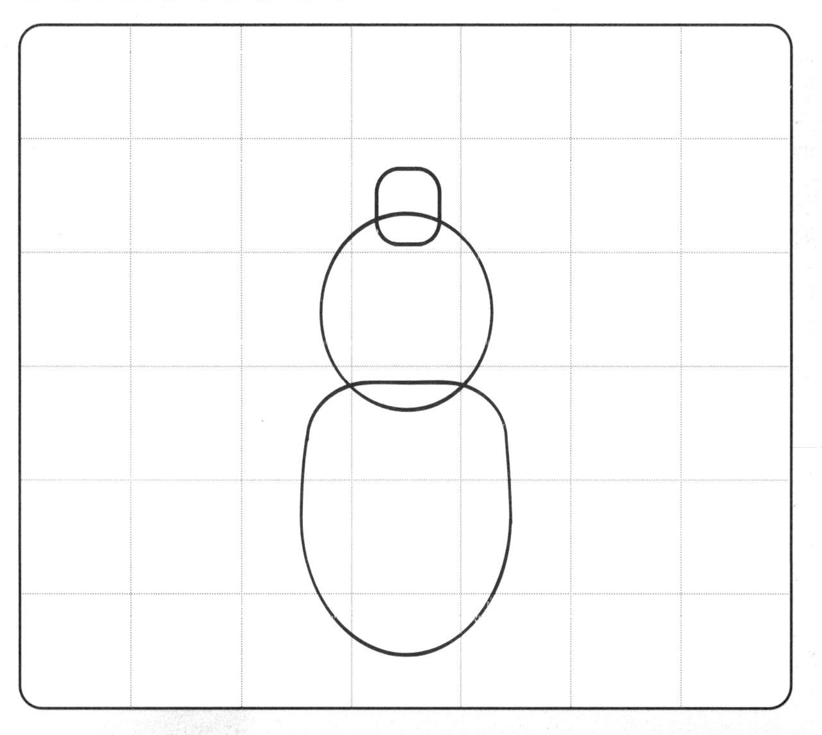

Step 1

Step 2

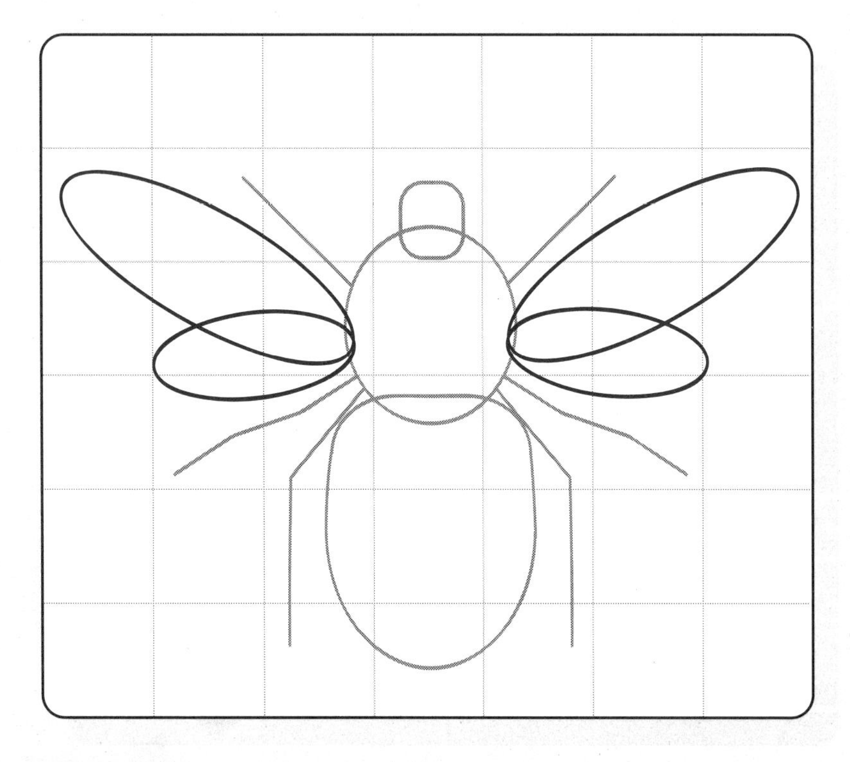

Step 3

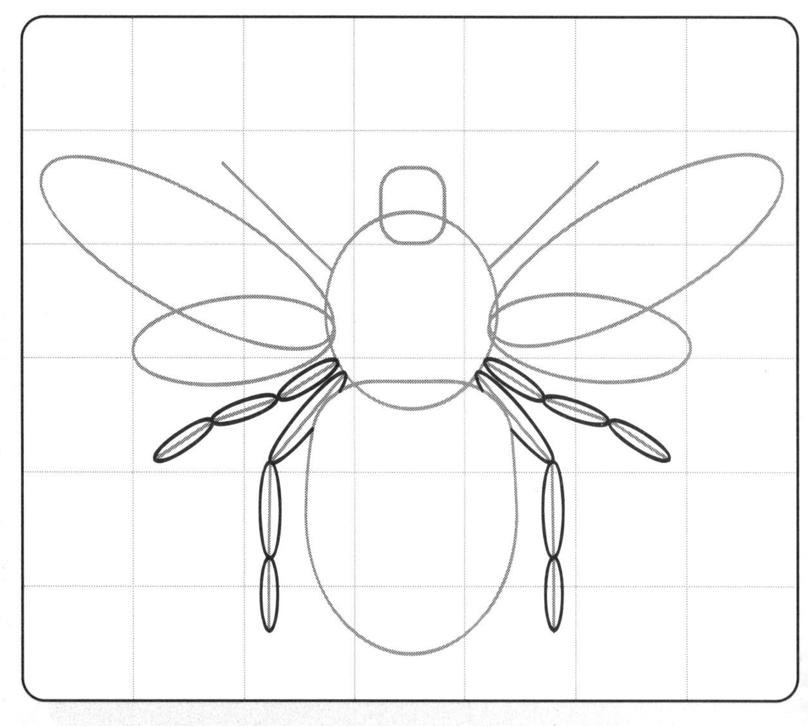

Step 4

Step 5

Step 6

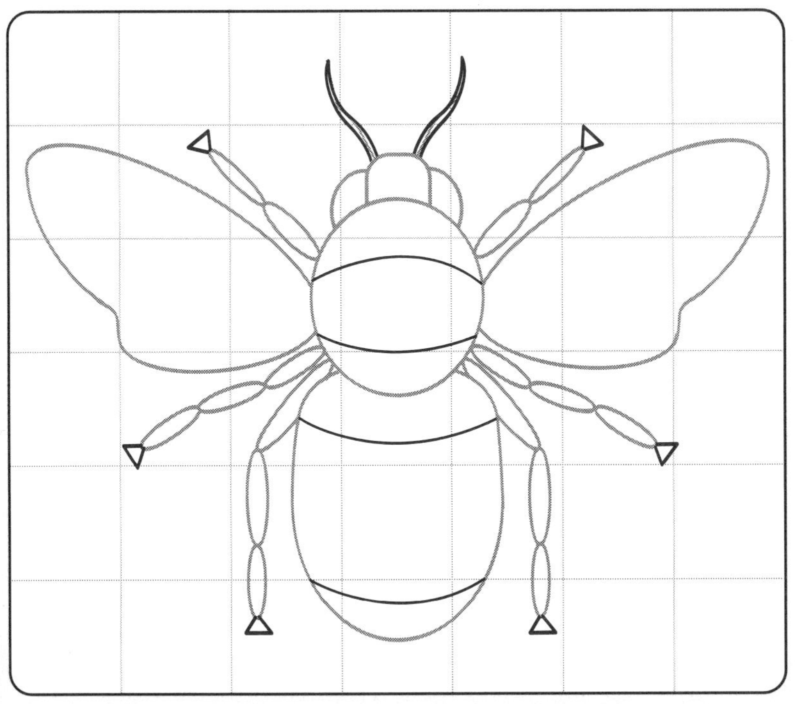

Step 7

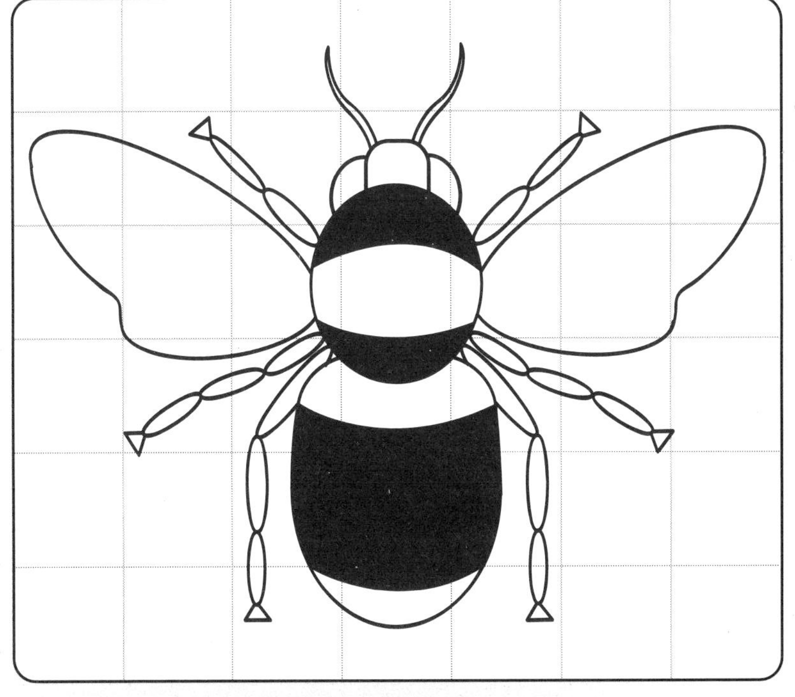

Step 8

Butterfly

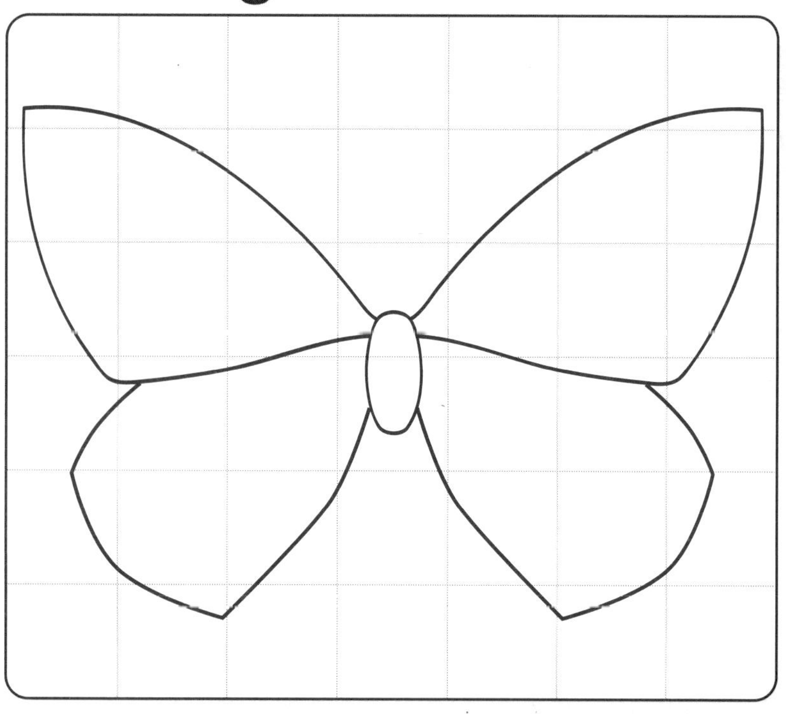

Step 1

Step 2

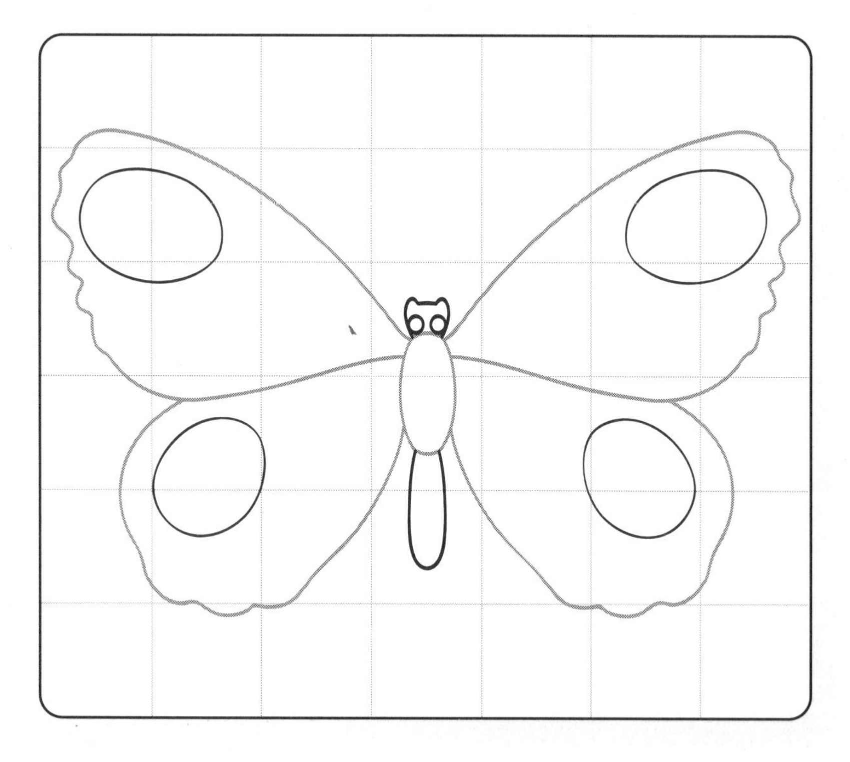

Step 3

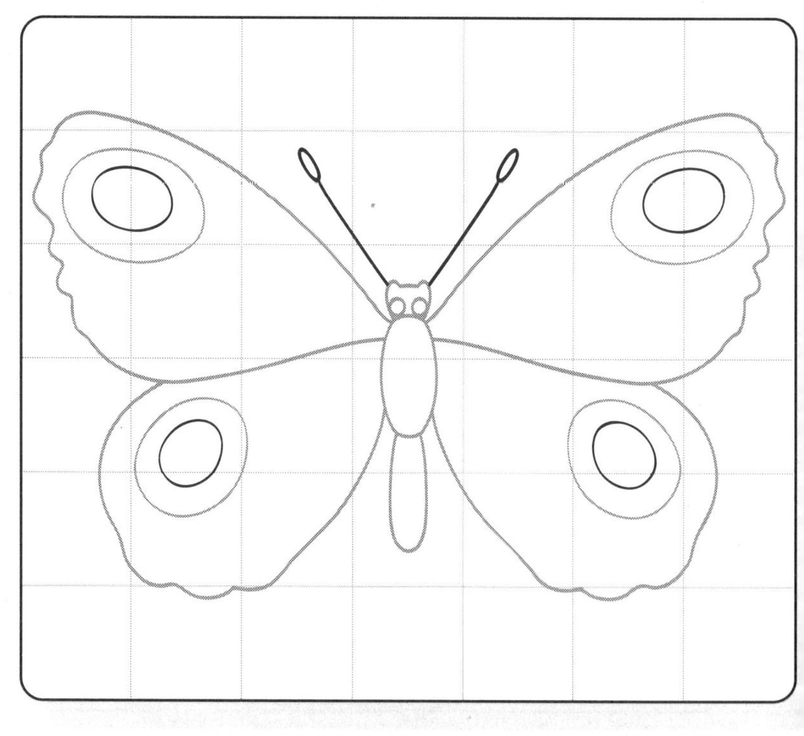

Step 4

Step 5

Step 6

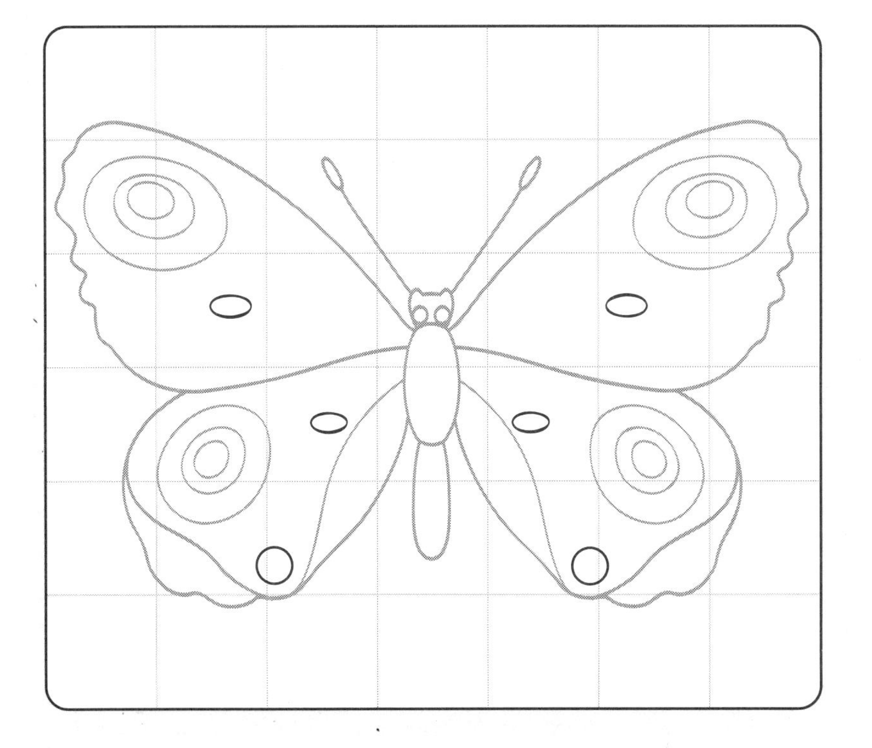

Step 7

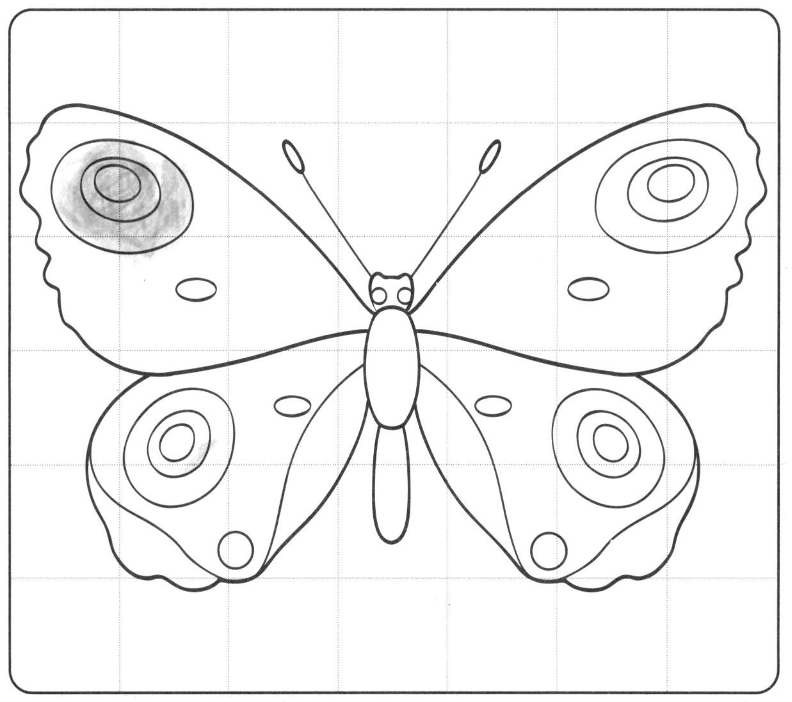

Step 8

Grasshopper

Step 1

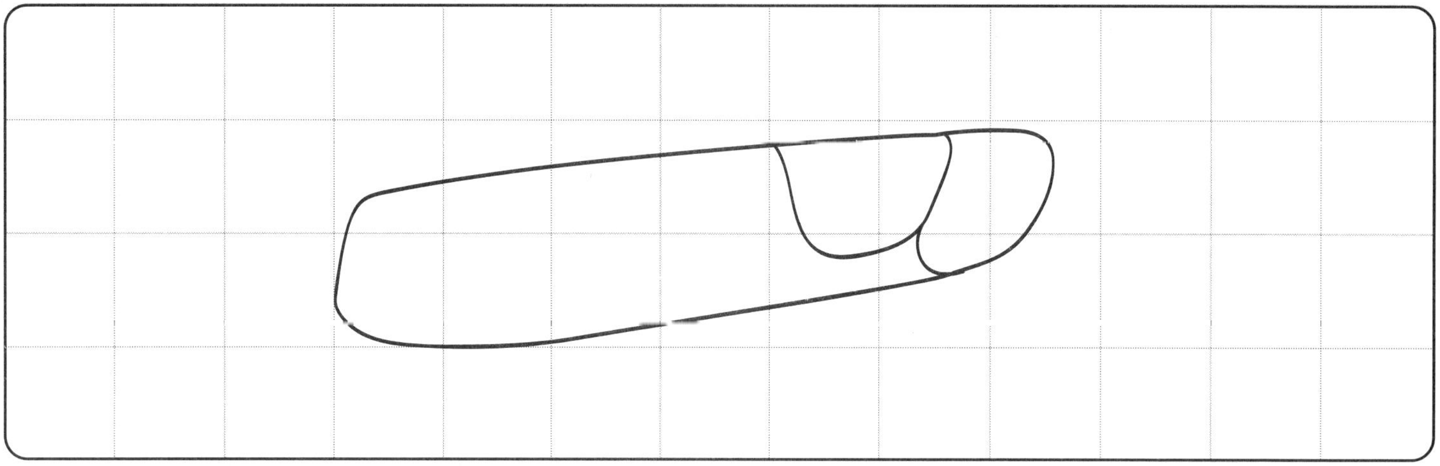

Step 2

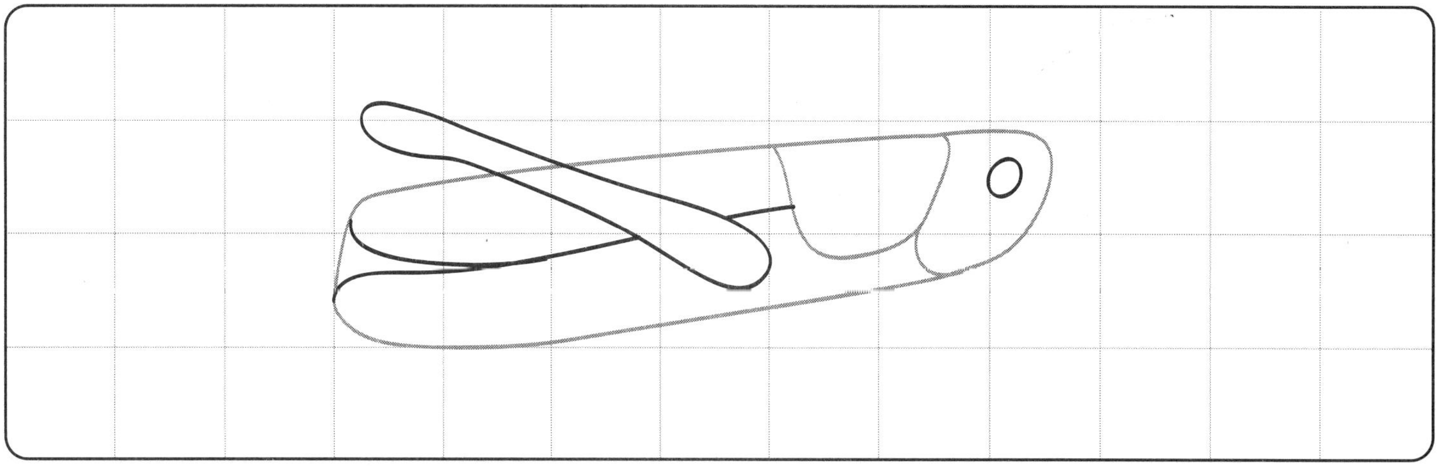

Step 3

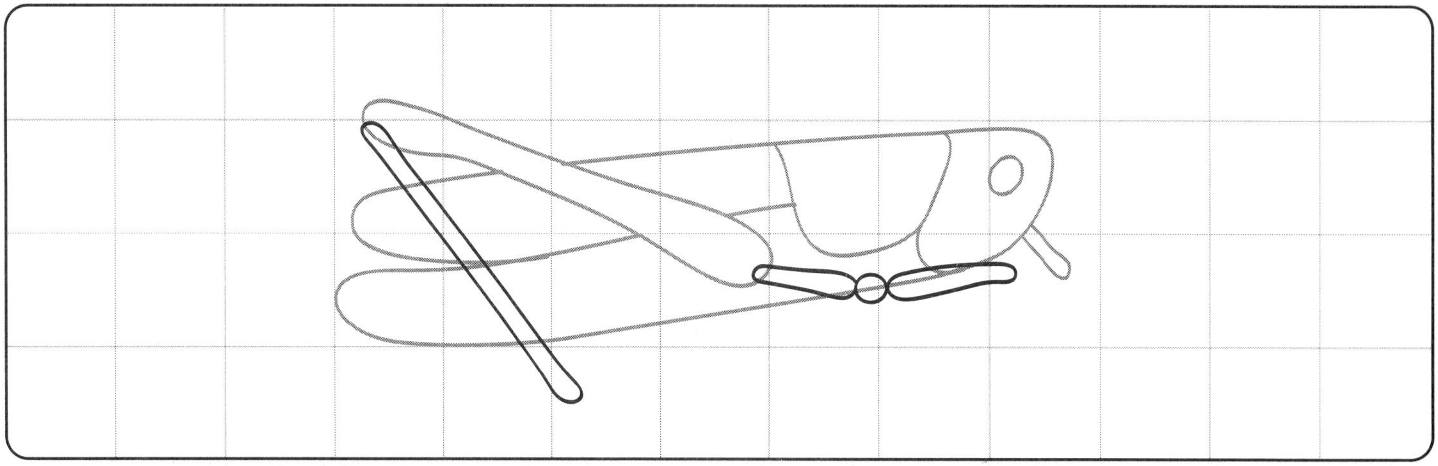

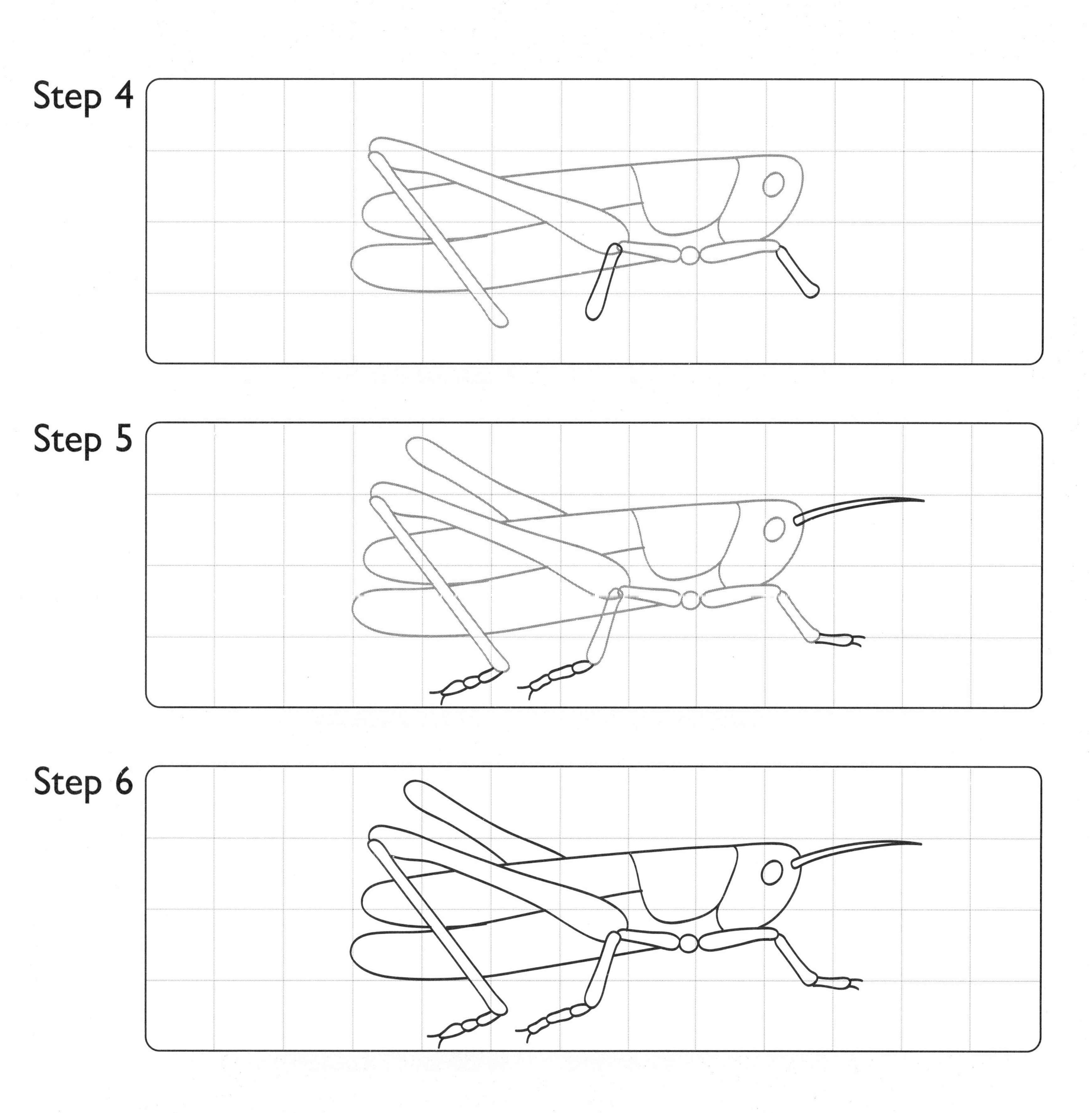
Step 4
Step 5
Step 6

KINGFISHER
a Houghton Mifflin Company imprint
222 Berkeley Street
Boston, Massachusetts 02116
www.houghtonmifflinbooks.com

First published in 2008
10 9 8 7 6 5 4 3 2 1
1TR/1107/THOM/IGS(SCHOY)/120BLT/C

Produced for Kingfisher by The Peter Bull Art Studio

For Kingfisher:
Associate creative director: Mike Davis
Designers: Ray Bryant and Emy Manby
Senior production controller: Jessamy Oldfield
DTP manager: Nicky Studdart

LIBRARY OF CONGRESS CATALOGING-IN-PUBLICATION DATA
Quick draw: creepy-crawlies.—1st ed.
p. cm.
ISBN-13: 978-0-7534-6198-3
1. Insects in art—Juvenile literature. 2. Animals in art—Juvenile literature. 3. Drawing—Technique—Juvenile literature. I. Title: Creepy-crawlies.
NC783.Q53 2008
743.6—dc22
2007031944

ISBN 978-0-7534-6198-3

Printed in India